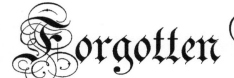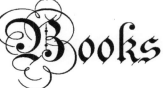

ISBN 978-1-334-03971-3
PIBN 10633276

This book is a reproduction of an important historical work. Forgotten Books uses
state-of-the-art technology to digitally reconstruct the work, preserving the original format
whilst repairing imperfections present in the aged copy. In rare cases, an imperfection in
the original, such as a blemish or missing page, may be replicated in our edition. We do,
however, repair the vast majority of imperfections successfully; any imperfections that
remain are intentionally left to preserve the state of such historical works.

1 MONTH OF
FREE
READING

at
www.ForgottenBooks.com

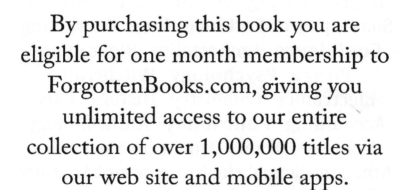

By purchasing this book you are eligible for one month membership to ForgottenBooks.com, giving you unlimited access to our entire collection of over 1,000,000 titles via our web site and mobile apps.

To claim your free month visit:
www.forgottenbooks.com/free633276

English
Français
Deutsche
Italiano
Español
Português

www.forgottenbooks.com

Mythology Photography **Fiction** Fishing Christianity **Art** Cooking Essays Buddhism Freemasonry Medicine **Biology** Music **Ancient Egypt** Evolution Carpentry Physics Dance Geology **Mathematics** Fitness Shakespeare **Folklore** Yoga Marketing **Confidence** Immortality Biographies Poetry **Psychology** Witchcraft Electronics Chemistry History **Law** Accounting **Philosophy** Anthropology Alchemy Drama Quantum Mechanics Atheism Sexual Health **Ancient History** **Entrepreneurship** Languages Sport Paleontology Needlework Islam **Metaphysics** Investment Archaeology Parenting Statistics Criminology **Motivational**

APHAEL SANTI

His Life and His Works

BY ALFRED BARON VON WOLZOGEN

TRANSLATED BY

F. E. BUNNÈTT

TRANSLATOR OF GRIMM'S 'LIFE OF MICHAEL ANGELO' AND GERVINUS'S
'SHAKESPEARE COMMENTARIES

LONDON
SMITH, ELDER, & CO., 65 CORNHILL
1866

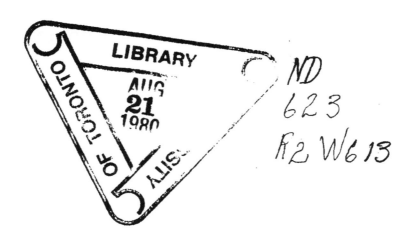

TRANSLATOR'S PREFACE.

HAVING translated Grimm's 'Life of Michael Angelo,' I was desirous of finding some memoir of his great contemporary Raphael, which might complete the picture we already possess of a period so rich in the history of Art.

It was not easy to meet with a work which was not too diffuse in its art-criticisms for the ordinary reader, and until Wolzogen's 'Life of Raphael' appeared, there was no concise biography of the great painter which seemed to me to supply the information required.

It is for this reason that I have translated the work; and I trust it will not be without interest to those who have hitherto known Raphael in his art alone.

F. E. BUNNÈTT.

PREFACE.

—◆—

RAPHAEL-LITERATURE already fills a library of its own. Extensive works, such as Passavant's ' Rafael von Urbino und sein Vater Giovanni Santi ' (three volumes, with maps, Leipsic, 1839-58), are among its treasures; but there is ever lacking a concise summary of all the more important investigations and decisions hitherto arrived at with regard to the great master's life and works. The best and most spirited of these are for the most part, moreover, in various papers and pamphlets, in which Raphael is not the sole subject. Passavant has only partially availed himself of this fragmentary material, and when he has done so, it has been, in my opinion, in such a manner as to admit at times of a different comprehension. So much, too, has appeared since the death of this industrious author, which deserves to have a place in a biography of Raphael. Lastly, all the works upon this master, even the most complete, have, it appears to me, laid too little stress upon his mission as regards the history of civilisation, and upon the importance of his art both philosophically and historically, although Schelling long ago drew attention to the subject.

This, therefore, must be my apology for the publication of the present work. It originated in four lectures, which I delivered for the Society for the History of the Plastic Arts. Raphael's public is large: it was my aim to furnish, as far as was possible, a complete picture of the great master, without overloading the portrait with too many detailed discussions. If, therefore, much has been in consequence omitted, which is of great interest to the special enquirer, I yet ndulge the hope of having afforded to those readers who desire from me neither an historical novel, nor a work based on new archival investigations, an insight into much which every cultivated man of the present day must desire to know respecting Raphael.

I have affixed to the end of the book rather a full Appendix; and I would draw the reader's attention to it, as it contains not only accurate statements of my authorities, but many opinions, differing from those usually received, are here more closely entered into.

A. VON WOLZOGEN.

BRESLAU: January 1865,

CONTENTS.

CHAPTER IV.

RAPHAEL IN ROME UNDER POPE JULIUS II.

1508–1513.

CHAPTER V.

RAPHAEL UNDER LEO X.

1513–1520.

CHAPTER VI.

CONCLUDING REMARKS.

RAPHAEL SANTI.

CHAPTER I.

INTRODUCTION.

In the history of the different arts, certain favoured individuals come conspicuously forward, who, from some especial gift of nature, are able to conceive and to carry out the highest tasks of that art whose votaries they are; their productions, therefore, form the culminating point of that art; but such men only appear when the art itself has gone through successive stages of development—stages which seem to a certain extent summed up in their works, and united in them into a perfect whole. These men form the central point of this development; all the earlier efforts of the art converge in them, and they appear to posterity as models, in whom the art has found the highest expression of its ideas that the progress of the age would admit of. The widening stream of life may present, in the future, tasks more comprehensive still for art to achieve; but we shall ever look back upon those stars of light and guidance as examples, in whom we may perceive that perfect harmony of all the elements of life, which found in them its expression and ideal image.

As in all individual development, there is a period at which the man reaches his highest stage of perfection, compared with which the past appears only as a time of preparation and the future one of retrogression; so, too, art has its highest point, at which its utmost power and ability are displayed. The characteristic of both these analogous conditions lies in the perfect unbroken power of the physical and intellectual life, in a state of pure harmony with the conscious mental principle in its phase of equal development. There is an incongruity, on the contrary, in the earlier and subsequent life: in the one the life of sense predominates, in the other that of the mind; the one is full of the impulses of life, without the power of representing them; the other exhibits the prevalence of reflection and study, while the producing power gradually disappears or exhausts itself in works which, in spite of all grandeur of conception, ay, in spite of all the fulness and vigour of life which they exhibit, fail in perfect beauty, because either the prevailing idea contained in them has completely absorbed everything that would affect the senses, or this has counterbalanced the force of the idea.

These general remarks might be illustrated by the history of any of the different arts, for these, being the highest forms of civilisation, necessarily reflect the process laid down by nature for the cultivation of man. In such an examination, we should see the highest points of the various branches of art attained by individual men who, equally favoured by natural gifts and by the circumstances of life, have approached most nearly to the pure conception of beauty; men who have created in their art a standard imagined by their predecessors, but no longer attainable by their posterity. Such men, therefore, stand forth as singular phenomena: all the fermenting and chaotic masses of ideas, struggling for form, order, and harmony, reveal themselves to them in magic beauty as in a mirror; the views and forms which a whole age endeavoured to obtain amid dim and irreconcilable ideas, become for the first time fully demonstrated in their works; and these works, bathed in the very ether of beauty, exercise a lasting influence upon the minds of all ages. That perfection to which Sophocles carried the tragic art of the Greeks was attained by none after him; and even Euripides, who was held in such esteem for his power of reflection, for his wonderful ability to excite and affect the mind of his audience, and for his impressive ease and magnificence of language, even he, in spite of these brilliant qualities, falls far short of the artistic beauty of his predecessor. In the kingdom of sound, Mozart stands forth as the type of perfect harmony, because his universal gifts, his never-failing instinct for art, joined to his inexhaustible ability for work, allowed him not merely to give expression to the various feelings of the mind, but to combine them harmoniously into one united whole.

A similar position in the sphere of painting, I feel compelled to claim for Raphael: the universal and therefore harmonious character of his mind was capable of receiving all that art had obtained in the course of its development; and, penetrating to the utmost the various sources of culture and learning of his age, he brought them, purified and refined, to bear on his own undying works—works, in which, as it were, a mighty past is concluded and a new epoch begins, and which, at the same time, as the purest symbol of a life purified and satisfied in itself, are able to exercise an imperishable influence upon all nations, all forms of faith, and all directions of taste.

If we would seek a parallel, none seems certainly more fitting than that between Raphael and Mozart. Rochlitz and Alberti have already drawn such a parallel,* and it is sanctioned also by Otto Jahn at the close of his biography of Mozart.† These are his words:— 'That noble beauty which seems, as it were, to absorb all other conditions of artistic representation, and to resolve itself into pure harmony, appears so equally triumphant in the works of these two masters, that, had we not so many points in accordance in the history óf their life and education, and in their artistic and moral nature, we should still scarcely fail to recognise them as twin brothers.' They were both 'animated by the spirit of truth, which breathes the breath of life into the soul;' both were 'conscientious in serious work, and playful in the freedom of invention.'‡ Their one love was the production of that exalted beauty in which, according to Schelling's profound expression, 'the richness of the form cancels the form itself.'

Winckelmann compares beauty with water, which,

---

* See Appendix, note i.   † See Appendix, note ii.
‡ See Appendix, notes iii. and iv.

drawn from the depths of the spring, is esteemed salubrious in proportion to its tastelessness. This highest kind of beauty we might designate the characterless, just in the same way as we say that 'the universe has no definite limit, neither length, nor breadth, nor depth, because it comprehends all in equal infinity; or that the art of creative nature is formless, because it is itself subject to no form.' We might call it characterless, therefore, in the same sense as that in which we regard Hellenic art in its highest stage, as exalted into the characterless, not having directly striven after it, for it far rather wrestled with the bonds of nature for this divine freedom. It is this highest kind of beauty, that is *ideal* beauty, which is only produced as the ripest fruits of the *characteristic* style, and yet which must acknowledge the characteristic as its real foundation and root—as its 'skeleton,' as it were;—for 'form cannot be without substance, and wherever form is, character is there also in visible or in merely sensible presence.' It is this beauty which Raphael and Mozart have pourtrayed and represented in a manner far superior to all other modern artists. 'It could have been,' says Schelling, 'no lightly scattered grain, but a deeply-seated seed, which could have produced such a mighty growth. It is only strong emotion of feeling, it is only a deep affecting of the imagination by the sense of the all-animating, all-governing forces of nature, which could bestow on art that invincible power with which it ever adhered faithfully to truth, in its course from the stiff reserved seriousness of the works of an earlier age, to those overflowing with the grace of feeling, investing the creations of the mind with the highest reality which is granted to mortals to behold.'

All those who, by the study of the characteristic style of art, have risen to the simplicity and sublimity of the so-called high style, must necessarily at some time have passed through that epoch to which, among the ancients, the tragedy of Æschylus belongs, and which was marked by the severe hard style of the plastic art, exhibited in the serious goddess Athene. ' In the statues of the most perfect or divine natures,' says Schelling, further, ' not only the utmost variety of forms, of which human nature is capable, ought to be combined, but the combination should also be of such a kind as we might imagine in the universe itself, the lower or those with lesser qualities under the higher, and all at length drawn up under *one* highest, in which, as it were, they lose their individuality, though in power and substance they still exist. If, therefore, we designate this high and self-sufficing beauty not characteristic, in so far as regards the limitation of the effect, still the characteristic element operates indiscernibly in its production, just as in crystal, transparent as it is, the texture nevertheless exists; every characteristic element influences, however gently, and helps to produce the sublime harmony of beauty.'

It was just this stage of development which was reached by art at the period of its renaissance in Italy, at the close of the Middle Ages. Schelling demonstrates this in a spirited manner, bringing forward Michael Angelo, Correggio, Raphael, and others, as examples. Some of what he has there said I may be allowed to repeat here, as I cannot better characterise the position of the artist, who is to be the subject of my consideration, among the other heroes of painting. I am glad also of this opportunity of drawing the attention of men of æsthetic taste to the almost forgotten paper by that profound philosopher, ' Ueber das Verhältniss der bildenden Künste zu der Natur.' I have borrowed the following extracts from it, for in it the true difference between ideal and characteristic beauty was first clearly presented to us, and upon this distinction our judgment in all matters of art essentially depends.

'Michael Angelo,' says Schelling,* 'represents the earliest and mightiest epoch of free art—that epoch in which in vast productions it displays its yet unfettered power. As in the allegorical poems of the old world, the Earth brought forth Titans and heaven-storming giants at the embrace of Uranus, before the soft rule of the peaceful deities began, so the work of the Last Judgment—with which, as the essence of his art, that giant mind filled the Sistine Chapel—seems to remind us rather of the early ages of this earth and their offspring, than of modern times. Attracted by the most secret principles of organic and especially of human structure, he never avoided the terrible; he sought it, indeed, intentionally, and roused it from its repose in the dark workshops of nature. Seriousness of character and a natural power of thought must have governed him far more than a perception of grace and a sensibility of feeling, in thus blending the highest attainments of pure plastic art with the painting of modern times.

* See Appendix, note v.

'When this first feeling of power is calmed and the
violent birth-throes stilled, then the rough spirit of
nature transforms itself into a feeling soul, and grace
bursts into life.   Art arrived at this stage after Leonardo da Vinci's death through Correggio, in whose
works the sensuous side of beauty is exhibited.   Not
only is this apparent in the delicate outlines of his
figures, but also in his forms, which are for the most
part similar to those of a purely sensuous nature in
the works of the ancients.   The general expression of
this appeal to the senses is the chiaroscuro, which was
brought to greater perfection by Correggio than by any
other painter.

'When the barriers of nature are overcome—when
the love of the vast, the fruit of the first freedom, is
done away with—form and figure become beautified by
the instinctive yearnings of the soul; heavenly light
descends; and the soothed earthly forms combine with
the heavenly, and these again with all that is sweetly
human.   Raphael takes possession of the bright
Olympus, and carries us away from earth to the assembly of the gods—beings permanent and blessed.
The prime of the most cultivated life, the sweet fra-
grance of imagination, and the vigorous power of mind,

all breathe forth from his works. He is no longer a painter ; he is at once a philosopher and a poet. His wisdom equals the power of his mind, and things are ordered in the everlasting decrees just as he pourtrays them. In him, art has reached its goal; and as the human and divine can be purely balanced at *one* point alone, the stamp of uniqueness is impressed on his works.'

In a similar manner, only dwelling more on the contrast between the *beautiful* and the *sublime,* than upon that between the *ideal* and the *characteristic,* Vischer speaks of the uniqueness of Raphael, as displaying the purest style of Italian painting, adorned with all the sweetness of grace. 'Raphael,' he says,* 'as regards the fundamental source of the beautiful, stands allied to the simply *beautiful* in contrast with the *sublime*; as regards the different stages of style, he belongs to the *charming* and *touching* style in contrast with the *high* style; and as regards the tendency of his painting, he takes the line of the relatively picturesque in contrast to that of the plastic art. But standing on his own platform, he grasps the form before him with a depth and breadth and fulness very different to that which Michael Angelo had done from his opposite

* See Appendix, note vi.

point of view: he opens what had been closed before, where the elements of the Divine had dwelt as the secret life of love, and he brings it into rich action and full energy of character: strong human souls in strong frames step forth to the storm and excitement of action, the spirit within acting as a mighty power; and from the representation of the contest he raises us to the enthroned majesty of divine greatness, and to the pure atmosphere of marvellous inspiration. Raphael is not merely the painter of calm, touching, lovely Madonnas, of Holy Families, and of charming boy-angels, but equally so of powerful and animated action, and, at the same time, of the highest glorification and imaginative grasp of that ideal, which he raised above everything earthly in the persons of Christ and the Virgin, and which he followed as no other had done through every stage. Thus, then, we cannot rank him as belonging to the charming and touching style in *contrast* to the high style, but he *united* the high style with it; although this high style, when exclusively followed, as by Michael Angelo, obtains a degree of power which is not possible in that harmony, in which the sublime itself is beautiful, and which a Raphael could scarcely have desired. That unity of grace and dignity which we found in Leonardo da Vinci, is extended in Raphael to an entire world, but in this world grace prevails, prevails even over dignity.'

Raphael's genius is here undoubtedly assigned its true place in the history of art. He stands absolutely and alone at the culminating point of painting. This, however, does not exclude the fact, that though beauty rests essentially in the just normal relation of things, in which all the efforts of the mind appear in equal harmony, these efforts may be exhibited with more intensity and effect, when separately pursued by other artists. It does not exclude the fact, I say, that Michael Angelo may be grander, Correggio more sweet and tender, even Guido Reni perhaps more spiritual, than Raphael; and that others may have brought other points of art *relatively* to greater perfection than he has done: just as, referring again to the analogy of music, Beethoven may have surpassed Mozart in pure instrumental music, and in the representation of that mighty power which makes *all* the strings of the human heart vibrate equally; and Gluck may have attained in his operas now and then to a strain of the simplest, holiest, and highest sublimity, not to be found in the works of Mozart. Nevertheless, such a consideration cannot drive either Raphael or Mozart from their true position. For those high qualities, which secure to *other* artists their well-deserved rank for all ages, are never felt as lacking in these two men; nay, they appear rather in them to be merely adjusted, and as it were glorified, by that central idea of beauty, which could not but allow them on some points a more limited sphere of action than was enjoyed by those whose productions bear not the stamp of perfect beauty to the same extent.

One more important point may be shown, in which Raphael's universally acknowledged greatness wonderfully agrees with Mozart's. I will here quote a beautiful passage of Göthe's, to be found in his 'Einzelheiten, Maximen und Reflexionen.' 'Raphael,' he says,* 'is the purest of modern artists. He is thoroughly *naïve*; the actual never comes with him into conflict with the moral or the sacred. The canva on which he has depicted the Adoration of the Kings, an exceedingly magnificent composition, represents an entire world, from the oldest of the adoring kings to the Moors and apes, amusing themselves on the camels with apples. The holy Joseph is here most

* See Appendix, note vii.

naïvely characterised as foster-father, delighting over the gifts received.' What does Göthe mean by this? The word 'naïveté' may be easily misunderstood with respect to artistic work, and we should fall into great error if we were to identify it with labourless production. The work of those artists whom we call naïve, is in nowise one of no labour; but that which is produced by them, has the effect of having been done without labour, and in this lies its marvellous power. A famous diplomatist once expressed himself thus: 'The greatest masterpiece of diplomatic art is to make men believe what they wish to believe.' The same expression will avail us here; and we may say, with the same justice: that artist stands at the highest point of his art, who by his works makes us believe in *that* beauty which we each unconsciously recognise as such. We can, however, only influence men in those beliefs, the germs of which lie already within them. 'Pensez-vous,' says the Père Lacordaire most eloquently in his 'Conférences' in Notre-Dâme in Paris,* 'pensez-vous que j'aurais le don de vous faire croire en Dieu, si le germe de cette croyance ne vivait pas au fond de votre cœur? De même que nulle force

* See Appendix, note viii.

chimique ne peut tirer des corps que les éléments qu'ils renferment, de même cette grande alchimie de la persuasion ne peut susciter dans notre esprit que des vérités indigènes; et si les livres sacrés ont pris possession du monde, c'est que le monde portait dans son sein des traditions sacrées dont ces livres ne sont que l'expression plus ou moins pure, plus ou moins corrompue. Tout livre sacré est livre traditionnel; on le vénérait avant qu'il fût, il existait avant de naître.' Now perfectly analogous with the books which we designate as sacred, is the case of those revelations of the highest genius which we call naïve. With all the artistic labour which they have bestowed on the creation of their works, they still appear, inasmuch as they have been created without reflection, not as anything artistically produced, but as the expression of a certain original type of the beautiful, the true, and the good, which has for ages slumbered yearningly in every soul. We see them, and we exclaim involuntarily, 'How have I imagined, painted, or chiselled this in my own soul!' Its mere existence is enough to convince every one of its genuineness. For such manifestations of original genius possess this too in common with the sacred writings, that no attacks made upon them lessen on the whole our faith in them. A man may write what he will against the Bible, but it ceases not to be the Book of Books for the Christian world, that book on which all the civilisation of the present day depends; a man may find fault as he will with Homer, Raphael, Shakespeare, Göthe, and Mozart, but they still remain as they are—*unalterably great*. And because it demands no special effort to believe in their excellence and uniqueness, the unbiassed critic, that is, he who is uninitiated in the mysteries of artistic work, feels himself inclined to suppose that the artists who have produced such works, have produced them without any effort. How often do we not hear the opinion expressed of productions such as these, which have received the enthusiastic applause of centuries, 'There is really no art in this; I could have done just the same!' Now, when such a verdict is uttered in simplicity, we may be assured that the highest art has been reached. Göthe says in his 'Zahmen Xenien':

Yes, this is the course we go:
That we do not know
When we think,
What we think—
Like a gift the thoughts do flow.

C

Such is the poetic interpretation of the impression produced upon us by works of art of the highest or naïve style. They appear to us as if inspired, as if they had originated by mere intuition; or, to use an expression employed in one of the fictitious letters published under Raphael's name, ' as if produced in a pleasant dream.'* The artist seems never during his work to have thought of tormenting his brains as to the manner of his representation, and therefore the author of the letter alluded to, makes Raphael say, ' During my work I have always thought more of the subject than of hów I should represent it.' By this, however, we only mean that the master completely entered into the subject of his work, and that the means for pourtraying this subject presented themselves to him naturally. And hence we always feel inclined to consider that supremacy which Raphael exercised over all minds, a supremacy bordering on the marvellous, not as the necessary result of his own laborious effort, but as the glorious reward of his innate personal amiability, and as a free gift which heaven bestows on its especial favourites, in common

* See Appendix, note ix.

with physical beauty and a life free from struggle and earthly misery. Still, however, we may suppose a long and continuous process of development in Raphael's case, and this to a far higher extent than is ordinarily conceded; for no artistic perfection is attained at a trifling cost; and he who, like Raphael, arrives at that rare freedom which makes the thing *acquired* appear as if *naturally produced,* must necessarily have laboured more, and more successfully in its completion, than others.* But then the capacity for this successful work must have dwelt within him, for many torment themselves with much endeavour without ever reaching any definite aim, and it is left for genius alone to pronounce everywhere and for ever its Cæsarian, 'Veni, vidi, vici.'

In indicating the main basis on which Raphael's wonderful individuality rests, the words occur to me which Anton Springer expressed in a public lecture delivered at Bonn on February 8, 1860:—'No artist's life passed so completely and immediately in artistic work as Raphael's. The essence of the beautiful seems indeed to have belonged to him as a personal quality.' †

---

* See Appendix, note x. † See Appendix, note xi.

He never felt those burdens of life which so often impede human effort. Because *we*, on the contrary, as work-day natures, can only rise at times to that perfect purity of soul mirrored in all the creations of Raphael— because in *our* restless striving we are thrown into the hard rude contrarieties of daily life, while an eternal holiday-mood prevailed with him, *our* æsthetic perceptions may turn to various other men in the history of art, as to more kindred natures; but if we at length attain to true peace of heart, we shall then find repose in the depth of those spiritual beings, free from struggle and desire, created for eternity by the *divine* mind of Raphael, for such it was designated by his admiring contemporaries.

With this opinion, with this supposition, who would undertake to delineate such a character even in its general features? I shall content myself, therefore, with calling to remembrance the outline of his outward life. A complete æsthetic estimate of the great master cannot be thus afforded, but it will furnish a basis for this, while it intimates the principal circumstances of his life.

CHAPTER II.

CHILDHOOD—EDUCATION—AND FIRST ATTEMPTS.

1483-1504.

THE SANTI FAMILY—BIRTH OF RAPHAEL—GIOVANNI SANTI—EARLY ATTEMPTS IN PAINTING—PERUGINO'S SCHOOL OF ART—RAPHAEL'S ASSOCIATES—HIS PAINTING AT PERUGIA—HIS RETURN TO URBINO—PAINTINGS FOR THE CITTÀ DI COSTELLA—RETURN TO PERUGIA—RAPHAEL LEAVES PERUGINO'S STUDIO—THE SPOSALIZIO—CHRIST ON THE MOUNT OF OLIVES—CARTOONS FOR PINTURICCHIO'S FRESCO PAINTINGS—ATTRACTED TO FLORENCE—LEONARDO DA VINCI AND MICHAEL ANGELO.

RAPHAEL, OR RAPHAELLO, as he himself wrote the name, sprung from a family, the eldest known ancestor of which, Sante by name, appears in the records of Colbordolo, a small town of Umbria, about the early part of the fourteenth century. His descendants received from him the family name *del Sante*, or *Santi*, and it was not until subsequently, in Vasari's time, that, according to Italian custom, the name was translated to *Sanzio*, from the Latin *Sanctius*. The great-grandson of that Sante was Giovanni Santi, the father of Raphael, who moved in the year 1450, with his grandfather Peruzzolo, to the larger city of Urbino, situated close to the highest summit of the Apennines, just where they separate the March of Ancona from Tuscany and Umbria. Here, in the Contrada del Monte, Raphael first saw the light, on Good Friday, March 28, 1483. He was the third of four children, who, however, all died young. His mother was Magia Ciarla, the daughter of a thriving merchant in Urbino; she died on October 7, 1491. On August 1, 1494, her son was left fatherless also. That Giovanni Santi was a good painter, the executor of many altarpieces in the churches throughout the March of Ancona, at Sinigaglia, Pesaro, Fano, and Montefiore, as well as in Urbino and in the surrounding neighbourhood, is equally well known as that he left behind him a rhyming chronicle, a biography in terzine of his honoured patron, the Duke Federico da Montefeltro, Lord of Urbino—a composition which is preserved in the Vatican among the Ottobonian manuscripts. At all events, these remains testify that Messer Giovanni held an honourable place among those highly cultivated artists of old, who were equally active with the brush and the pen. On May 25, 1492, he married Bernardina, the daughter of the goldsmith Pietro di Parte; but the character of his second wife was less affectionate than that of Magia, and after her husband's death she was a frequent cause of vexation to her stepson.

It is not to be doubted that Raphael received his first instruction in painting from his father, and that the latter himself perceived the great talent of his son. He took the boy with him in a journey he made to Cagli between 1492 and 1494, when he undertook the task of adorning with frescoes the family chapel of Pietro Tiranni, in the church formerly called St. John's, and now that of the Dominicans. These frescoes belong to his best works, and it is more than probable that Raphael had a helping hand in them. Nothing, unfortunately, has been preserved of Raphael's earliest independent attempts, and even any information respecting them in the old manuscripts at Urbino, is quite uncertain. It is said that, as a boy, he was employed in the decoration of the chapel of the Galli family in the church of San Francesco—a chapel now in ruins; that he painted an interesting picture, *a tempera*, in the monastery of Santa Chiara,

and other things—stories which are all just as indefi-
nite and devoid of authenticity, as that which has
been transmitted to us respecting his early training.

After the death of his father in 1494, he was
consigned to the care of his guardian and uncle, the
ecclesiastic Don Bartolommeo Santi, and to that of his
stepmother, neither of whom, however, knew how to
awaken the confidence of the tender-hearted child. His
affections turned principally to his uncle on the mother's
side, Simone di Battista Ciarla, whom throughout his
life he addressed in his letters as 'beloved like a father'
(Carissimo in locho de Patre), and whom he held
in hearty reverence. Luca Signorelli and Timoteo
Viti are mentioned as his first teachers in painting;
and the latter of these, returning to Urbino from
the atelier of Francesco Francia at Bologna, is said to
have painted the portrait of Raphael when twelve
years old—a picture now in the Borghese Gallery in
Rome.

It was probably in this same year that the boy was
placed in Perugia, under the instruction of Pietro
Vannucci della Pieve, called Perugino. This chief
master of the Umbrian school, whose character, according to Rumohr's striking expression, was marked

by 'stainless purity of soul, by the highest aspirations, 'and by feeling, sweetly sad and enthusiastically tender,' —this master had been the pupil of Niccolo Alunno of Fuligno and the Florentine Andrea Verrocchio; and now, standing on the highest pinnacle of his fame, he had gathered round him a great number of distinguished pupils. Raphael attached himself warmly to some of these, and soon surpassed them all. Among his especial associates were Andrea di Luigi of Assisi, called l'Ingegno, and Domenico di Paris Alfani, to whom Raphael gave a design in 1508 as a sketch for an altar-piece, which Domenico had to execute at Perugia.* There were besides, Cesare di Francesco Rossetti,† a famous goldsmith at Perugia, who is said to have instructed our artist in architecture, Gaudenzio Ferrari of Balduccio, many works of value by whom are preserved in the Milanese city Brera, and others. Raphael appears also to have been intimate at that time with Bernardino di Betti of Perugia, surnamed Il Pinturicchio, although the latter, having been born in 1454, and therefore only eight years younger than Perugino, who was born in 1446, could scarcely have

* See Appendix, note xii.   † See Appendix, note xiii.

been a pupil of that artist. Among the earliest works completed by Raphael at Perugia, there is a small picture, *a tempera,* with a gold ground, in imitation of a large altar-piece painted by Perugino for the church Santa Maria de' Fossi in that city. The picture represents Christ as a child with St. John, and it is still preserved as an interesting relic in the sacristy of the church San Pietro Maggiore at Perugia. The sketch-book in the academy at Venice contains other studies by Raphael after his master.

Very soon Perugino made use of his assistance in works of importance; his picture of the 'Birth of Christ,' which was formerly in the church of the Minori riformati della Spineta at Todi, and is now in the Vatican, decidedly betrays Raphael's hand, as does also the picture of the 'Resurrection of Christ,' painted for the church of the Franciscans at Perugia, but now likewise in the Vatican, and the six divisions of the altar-piece painted for the Certosa, near Pavia, and now partly in the possession of the Duca Melzi at Milan. In the first-mentioned picture, it is especially the head of Joseph, and in the last the two arch-angels Michael and Raphael with Tobias, which may be ascribed with certainty to the youthful Raphael.

In the year 1499, he returned to Urbino to settle
the disputes which had arisen between his stepmother
and guardian, and he had the delight of lastingly
restoring family peace by his sweet and gentle be-
haviour. He received his first independent order with
the beginning of the new century. The Città di
Castello commissioned him, as Messer Perugino had
gone to Florence on business, to paint a banner for
a procession, which is still preserved, and a Cruci-
fixion with four saints in adoration, for the church of the
Holy Trinity. This latter work came into the collection of Cardinal Fesch at Rome, and has been, since
1847, in Lord Ward's gallery in London. To these
may be added the order for a picture for the church of
St. Augustine in the same city,—the heavenly coronation
of the wonder-working hermit Nicholas of Tolentino—
a picture since destroyed—and also a commission
from the Gavari family to paint a large altar-piece
for their chapel in the church of the Dominicans at
Città di Castello, representing Christ on the Cross,
surrounded by the Virgin, St. John, Mary Magdalene,
and Hieronymus. This picture also fell into the possession of Cardinal Fesch, and subsequently into that
of Lord Ward.

After the completion of these works Raphael returned to Perugia, where he executed several pictures, large and small, entirely in Perugino's style. Among these we may number the small picture of the 'Madonna,' which passed from the Solly collection into the Berlin Museum; and also the 'Madonna' in the possession of the Countess Anna Alfani at Perugia; the 'Madonna with the Infant Christ;' 'St. Jerome and St. Francis,' in the collection of the Archduke Charles at Vienna; the now much damaged 'Adoration of the Magi,' painted for the Abbey Church at Ferentillo, between Spoleto and Terni, but in the Berlin Museum since 1825; and the 'Sleeping Knight,' attended by two allegorical female figures, one of whom, holding before him sword and book, calls him to undertake deeds of chivalry, while the other is extending flowers to him as a symbol of the sensual enjoyment of life. This picture is in the National Gallery in London. Among other works belonging to the same period, we may reckon a small painting of the Madonna in the Casa Connestabile at Perugia; some *predelli*, such as the 'Baptism and Resurrection of Christ,' from the Inghirami house at Volterra, now in the Pinakothek at Munich; the 'Adoration of the

Kings' in the castle of Christiansburg at Copenhagen; a half-length of St. Sebastian, in the possession of Count Guglielmo Lochis at Bergamo, and fifteen or sixteen more small paintings.[*]

It is to be supposed that in the year 1504, Raphael formally quitted Perugino's studio. He now again repaired to Città di Castello, where he painted for the church of the Franciscans the ' Sposalizio,' known to all the world by Longhi's engraving, and now the ornament of the Brera in Milan. In this picture we see Perugino's style and sense of beauty already really surpassed by the youth, who had so completely made them his own, although he still seems governed by the influence of his master.[†] Vasari justly points out that the circular temple surrounded with columns, seen in the background, must be regarded as a wonderful proof of the ease with which the young artist, even at that time, could conquer the greatest difficulties in perspective drawing. The style indeed of this architecture is so pure, all the details are so justly proportioned, and executed with such delicacy, that in this work we can scarcely fail to perceive the beginnings of an independent exercise of his genius.

[*] See Appendix, note xiv.   [†] See Appendix, note xv.

In the same year, Raphael again returned to his
native city, and painted some small pictures for Duke
Guidobaldo of Urbino. These paintings are, 'Christ
on the Mount of Olives'—a picture which, since the
year 1847, has been in the possession of Mr. W.
Fuller Maitland at Stanstead, in the county of Essex,
'St. George and the Dragon,' now in the Louvre, and
'St. Michael combating the Monster,' in the same
place. About this time Pinturicchio, who had been
entrusted by Cardinal Francesco Piccolomini, afterwards Pope Pius III., with the execution of the fresco
paintings in the library of the cathedral at Siena,
sent for Raphael to this city; and it is certain—not,
indeed, as Vasari falsely states in his 'Life of Pinturicchio,'* that he made *all* the sketches and cartoons for the fresco paintings of the mature master
of fifty years of age—but that he executed two larger
finished designs from the sketches of the latter, from
which, however, Pinturicchio deviated in some points
when he transferred them to the wall and coloured
them.† One cartoon, now in the Uffici, represents
Æneas Silvius Piccolomini accompanying Cardinal

* See Appendix, note xvi.   † See Appendix, note xvii.

Capranica to the Council at Basle; the other cartoon, in the possession of the Baldeschi family at Perugia, represents the meeting of the Emperor Frederic III. and his bride, Eleonora of Portugal, at the Porta Camollia at Siena.

Vasari relates that Raphael only discontinued his work in furnishing designs for Pinturicchio, because he heard from some artists in Siena the praise of the cartoon which the famous Leonardo da Vinci, at that time fifty-three years of age, had just completed for the fresco paintings of the Sala del Consiglio in the Palazzo Vecchio at Florence, in competition with that of Michael Angelo, then thirty years of age. The cartoon of the former represented an attack of cavalry in the contests between the Milanese and the Florentines; that of the latter a group of bathing soldiers summoned to the battle—an episode in the wars between Pisa and Florence: and both artists excelled especially in an art at that time almost unknown to the young Raphael — that of pourtraying the naked figure.

Quatremère de Quincy* has demonstrated in a few

* See Appendix, note xviii.

words what was the unusual power of attraction possessed by that new manifestation of Florentine art.
' To understand this well,' he says, ' we must form a
just idea of the method and style of drawing which at
that time prevailed, with few exceptions, in all the
schools. The customs of the time had not favoured
the study of the human body, nor had the prevalence
of religious subjects and the habits of religious decency
made it appear especially necessary. Equally little
had the statues of the antique, existing at that time in
so small a number, had any influence in bringing about
a perfect knowledge of the naked figure.* A certain
truth universally prevailed, but it never rose above
that which belongs to portrait painting. While similar
faces were preserved, the different costumes of the age
were copied with accuracy and routine. Whatever there
was of the naked figure, consisted of an outline of the
contour, without articulation, or any true arrangement
of the muscles. The ease of the drawing corresponded
with that of the composition. The painter was afraid
of venturing to select a scene requiring any contrast of
position, and exhibiting the human body in attitudes

* See Appendix, note xix.

more or less difficult to conceive, in manifold groups or complicated situations, by which a bold effect might be produced.'

This new acquisition of art was exhibited for the first time by the cartoons just mentioned. The study of the antique and of anatomy had broken through the old traditionary rules, and with the new resources thus afforded for picturesque representation, there went hand in hand the devising of new subjects, such as would never have been ventured upon by the more timid artists of the past and of his own day.

And could such a work, such an immense advance in art, be indifferent to a painter of Raphael's endowments and aspirations? Nay, it drew him irresistibly to Florence, although he had no mission there of any kind—and, indeed, probably brought with him no other recommendation than that which lay in his amiable and gifted nature.*

* See Appendix, note xx.

D

CHAPTER III.

RAPHAEL IN FLORENCE.

1504–1508.

MASSACCIO AND THE MODERN STYLE OF ITALIAN ART—RAPHAEL'S
IMPRESSIONS IN FLORENCE—POWER OF IMITATION IN DIFFERENT
ARTISTS—THE INFLUENCE OF THE FLORENTINE SCHOOL ON RAPHAEL
—HIS FIRST PAINTING IN FLORENCE—HIS RETURN TO PERUGIA—
HIS PAINTINGS THERE—THE ALTAR-PIECE AT BLENHEIM—RAPHAEL'S
RETURN TO FLORENCE—BACCIO D'AGNOLO—RAPHAEL GOES TO
BOLOGNA AND URBINO—SPLENDID COURT OF DUKE GUIDOBALDO—
'THE THREE GRACES'—RETURN TO FLORENCE—'THE ENTOMBMENT
OF CHRIST' AT PERUGIA—BACCIO DELLA PORTA—SUMMONED TO
ROME BY POPE JULIUS II.

ONE of the most striking proofs of the healthy nature
of Raphael's mind is the fact that, with all his marvellous capacity for learning and assimilation, he ever
avoided most carefully any leap in the regular progressive development of his genius.   Fortune may
have favoured him here also in an extraordinary
manner; at any rate, she smiled upon a worthy
disciple, and one specially called to attain perfection.

Tradition informs us that while in Florence he studied thoroughly, beyond all else, the works of Massaccio, the true founder of the modern school of Italian painting. This artist had been dead for more than half a century; but the efforts after life-like truth, characteristic expression, and natural simplicity —in a word, after that picturesque completeness in which the later Florentine artists excelled—are manifested in him most effectively.* If he did not, perhaps, possess the full power of the sublime, he towered far above the modest grace and tender feeling of the Umbrian school. Fine drawing, an accurate study of nature, composition, abundance of characters, individual distinctions, and animated action—all these stand out, in his famous fresco paintings in the church of the Carmelites at Florence, like a new revelation in art, making ready the way for the great deeds of Leonardo da Vinci and Michael Angelo, until Raphael at length, from his starting-point of pure beauty, grasped the whole, and led on to the perfection of art.

Mighty were the impressions which the youth received in beholding so much that was new; still,

* See Appendix, note xxi.

however, he did not at once disengage himself from
Perugino's style and the Umbrian school; and the
reason for this lay not only in his hearty reverence for
his master, and in his long use and thorough appropriation of the method of the latter, but especially in
the fact—a fact which will always distinguish true
genius from mere superficial talent—that it was impossible to him to become a mere formal copyist of
others.   If he would really learn from the Florentines,
and especially from the great Leonardo da Vinci, with
all his science and art—from that man who required
that the painter should carry the world in his mind
before he should undertake to represent it—he must
have gone through all that which Vasari describes.*
' When,' as Vasari says, ' he first saw Leonardo's works,
he stood before them perfectly amazed and astonished;
they pleased him at once better than all he had seen
before, and he felt, therefore, impelled to a deeper
study of them; but, in spite of this, it was only with
great effort and infinite labour that he succeeded in
leaving Perugino's style, and imitating that of Leonardo.'

* See Appendix, notes xxii. and xxiii.

Genius manifests itself in this also, that it alone possesses the capacity of adopting the individual style of a master and bringing it to still higher perfection, without allowing it to degenerate into mannerism. 'The pupil, on the other hand, who has neither genius nor inward call to become himself a master, in the full meaning of the word, propagates, it is true,' as .Vischer says,* 'the style of his master, but by degrees he lowers it to mere mannerism, because the genius is lacking which ought to [fill his figures. Thus the sweet smile in the female faces of Leonardo da Vinci has often become an affected simper with artists of the Milanese school; and thus both Michael Angelo's power and Correggio's grace and rapture have proved paths of decline, and a false style of power and a false mannerism of grace and sickly sentimentality have arisen. We must not, however, therefore suppose that the individual style, as soon as it passes into the hand of another, necessarily degenerates into mannerism; this happens only with pupils deficient in genius or in mental vigour, and still more in consequence of an unfavourable condition of things, when art in general

* See Appendix, note xxiv.

is on the decline. The skilful pupil, called as he is
himself to great achievements, carries on the style to
its perfection until he surpasses it, as Raphael did that
of Perugino. Before he displays his own independent
power, he may adopt for a short period the more
advanced style of another master; and this first style,
thus appropriated, corresponds with that which, with
other beginners (especially poets), is the stormy burst of
nature which belongs to the period of commencement.
Thus, in the course of Raphael's development, we
trace three stages of style—namely, that of his first
master Perugino, which marks his childhood; the *Florentine*, which belongs to the period approaching
maturity; and the *Roman*, which stamps his mature
works.'

Thus we find ourselves now at the commencement
of the second period in Raphael's career, in which,
joined to his incomparable genius and the great
correctness, grace, and tenderness of design he had
already attained, he displayed that peculiar warmth
of colouring which distinguishes the Umbrian school.
It was necessary for him now, in the first place, to
throw aside the restraint of his master Perugino—a
master exclusively absorbed in heavenly devotion and

in the glories of the next world, and bringing the ideal of fervent feeling alone to perfection—and, having done this, gradually to cultivate the other sides of painting, especially the representation of individual character and the variety of human life.

The 'Madonna del Granduca,' one of the first pictures painted by Raphael in Florence, has in it a tone somewhat grander than belonged to the sad dreamy paintings of the Perugino school. At about the same period also we may place the 'Madonna surrounded by Three Children,' a painting which belonged to the Duca di Terranuova, and was purchased by the Berlin Museum in 1855; the small hasty sketch of a Madonna, half life-size, in the possession of Lord Cowper at Penshanger in Hertfordshire, where the Virgin is sitting on a stone seat with her head inclined sideways, holding the infant Christ with her left hand, while the right rests on her lap, on which the child is standing with his arms round his mother's neck;* and, lastly, the portrait of a youth about eighteen or twenty years old, of the family of Leonardo del Riccio in Florence,† from which family King Lewis of Bavaria sprung.

---

* See Appendix, note xxv.   † See Appendix, note xxvi.

Many commissions compelled Raphael to return
to Perugia in the spring of 1505. He painted for
the convent of St. Anthony there, a piece for the
high altar, of which the principal composition was a
'Madonna with Four Saints,' and, in a semicircular frame
above, 'God the Father with Angels,' a painting now
in the royal palace at Naples. Besides these, he
painted a fresco in San Severo, representing the Holy
Trinity, and the beautiful and well-preserved Madonna
of the family of Filippo di Simone Ansidei, as an altar-
piece for the chapel of San Nicolo di Bari in the
church of San Fiorenzo dei P.P. Serviti at Perugia;
part of this altar-piece is now in the Duke of Marl-
borough's possession at Blenheim, and part is at
Bowood, the seat of the Marquis of Lansdowne. The
altar-piece at Blenheim represents the Virgin sitting on
a throne, ascended by three steps; she is holding the
Child on her lap with her right hand, and in the left
she has a small open book, on which the Child is gazing
with sweet seriousness. Close by on the left stands
John the Baptist, represented as a man holding in his
left hand a cross of glass reaching to the ground, and
pointing with his right hand to Christ. Nicholas of
Bari stands on the right in episcopal robes; in his left

hand he holds an open book, and in his right a golden
crosier. Three golden apples lie at his feet. A landscape, surrounded by an ornamented light grey arch,
forms the background. The figures are about three-
quarter size.* The centre picture of the predella
belonging to the above-described altar-piece is at
Bowood. It represents John the Baptist preaching,
but it is unfortunately in some parts much injured and
defaced.†

Raphael now, however, again returned to Florence,
for the narrow sphere of art at Perugia could no longer
satisfy his restless and onward striving mind. A distinguished circle of young and old artists were wont at
that time to assemble of an evening in the studio of
the architect and sculptor Baccio d'Agnolo.‡ Vasari
mentions among others Andrea Sansovino, Antonio
and Giuliano di Sangallo; even Michael Angelo Buonarotti is said to have been there sometimes. Much that
was beautiful and profound relating to art was discussed there; but Raphael expressed his ideas with
more fervour and eloquence than any, and won all
hearts by his power. Distinguished citizens of Florence,

---

* See Appendix, note xxvii.   † See Appendix, note xxviii.
‡ See Appendix, note xxix.

who also visited the house of Baccio d'Agnolo, became acquainted with him here; and for one of these, Lorenzo Nasi, he painted the 'Madonna del Cardellino' (with the goldfinch) in the Tribuna of the Uffizi at Florence, and for another, Taddeo Taddei, the learned friend of the Cardinal Pietro Bembo, who conceived a passionate affection for Raphael, he painted the 'Madonna,' now in the Imperial Palace at Vienna, and the 'Holy Family with the Fan-palm,' now in the Bridgewater Gallery.* Some portraits also belong to this period; among others, that of the rich merchant Angelo Doni and his wife Maddalena, now in the Pitti Palace; and that picture, unfortunately so much effaced, of a young unknown Florentine, with green bodice and white apron, in the Tribuna of the Uffizi, once pointed out as Maddalena Doni; and another portrait of a young Florentine lady. In the latter, a great advance in the technical part of the art is perceivable; it hangs in the Pitti Palace, and has been finely engraved by C. Vitta on a small scale. It is probable that at the beginning of this year, Raphael went to Bologna for the sake of becoming acquainted with Francesco Francia, and to

---

* See Appendix, note xxx.

paint an 'Adoration of the Shepherds' for the Governor of Bologna, Giovanni Bentivoglio. This painting, which was formerly at Ildefonso, has now disappeared.

From Bologna, our artist once more repaired to his native city Urbino, where Duke Guidobaldo had just gathered a brilliant court around him.* Here were to be found some of the most intellectual people of that day in Italy—Count Baldassare Castiglione, the most accomplished courtier, poet, and writer; Giuliano dei Medici, brother of Leo X.; Andrea Doria, the famous Genoese ; Pietro Bembo, afterwards Secretary to Leo X.; Bernardo Divizio da Bibbiena, subsequently Cardinal of Santa Maria in Portico, a man replete with wit and wisdom; and many others. Certain it is that the influence of these men upon Raphael was not inconsiderable; until his death he remained on terms of friendship with most of them. He still painted only small pictures for the Duke, as the latter was not rich; one of these was intended as a present to King Henry VII. of England, and was conveyed thither by Count Castiglione.† The subject was a ' St. George on Horseback killing the Dragon,' and the picture is now

---

* See Appendix, note xxxi.　　† See Appendix, note xxxii.

in the hermitage at St. Petersburg. He painted also two 'Madonnas' for the Duke; a 'Holy Family,' in which Joseph is represented without a beard; a picture, now also at St. Petersburg; and the so-called small 'Madonna' of the Orleans Gallery, now in the possession of M. Dellessert at Paris; besides the portraits of the Duke of Urbino and his wife Elizabeth, of which all trace is lost. In addition to these, he executed at the same time a portrait of Pietro Bembo in black chalk, which has likewise disappeared; his own well-known likeness, probably intended for his uncle Simone Ciarla, and now in the picture gallery of the Uffizi; and, lastly, the 'Three Graces,' a painting formerly in the Galleria Borghese at Rome, subsequently in that of Lord Dudley, and since 1850 in the possession of Lord Ward in London. The group is arranged completely in imitation of the antique. The dotted engraving of it by Sherwin is bad, but that done by Forster in Paris, in 1841, is very excellent. This charming picture, seven inches square, is so far well worthy of notice, in that it exhibits Raphael's first attempt in representing the naked figure, and displays a more direct influence from the antique than any of his previous works. With the exception of the lacking nymph, as

Giesebrecht justly points out, it corresponds throughout with those beautiful lines of Horace (Carm. iv. 7):—

> Diffugere nives, redeunt jam gramina campis
>   Arboribusque comæ :
> Mutat terra vices, et decrescentia ripas
>   Flumina prætereunt:
> Gratia cum Nymphis geminisque sororibus audet
>   Ducere nuda choros.
> Immortalia ne speres, monet annus et almum
>   Quæ rapit hora diem.

We may, moreover, conclude, with some degree of certainty, that this picture was suggested to Raphael during his residence in Siena by the beauty of the marble antique of the 'Graces,' which now stands in the Liberia of the cathedral at Siena. Here, also, the middle figure recedes, while the two others advance, and all three touch each other's shoulder with the one hand, while the other holds a golden ball, for throwing and catching during the dance. Their hair is adorned with bands of red coral, and the figure on the right has a necklace of the same, while that on the left has a band round her waist and thigh. The background is formed by a hilly landscape, in which even the stream of that ode of Horace is not missing. The countenances have that expression of melancholy sweetness which belongs to Perugino's school, and which is quite in harmony with the concluding words of the passage we have quoted.*

On his journey to Florence he painted on wood, *a tempera*, the portraits of two priests, Blasio and Don Baldassare, in the monastery of Vallombrosa. These portraits were placed in the Florentine Academy in 1813. Having arrived in Florence, he executed the beautiful painting of the ' Holy Family ' for Domenico Canigiani, which is now in the Pinakothek at Munich, though much effaced and painted over. This painting, which is so highly extolled by Vasari,† represented the Virgin, the Infant Christ, Joseph, Elizabeth, St. John, and two boy-angels ; the latter, however, were erased as superfluous by the Gallery Inspector at Düsseldorf, where the picture was placed for some time, and the space has been filled up with some grey clouds.‡

Soon after Raphael received the order from Atalante Baglioni to paint the ' Entombment of Christ ' for the Franciscan church at Perugia—a painting which now constitutes the principal ornament of the Galleria Borghese at Rome. This painting was completed at Perugia in the year 1507, after he had made the most

---

* See Appendix, note xxxiii.　　† See Appendix, note xxxiv.
‡ See Appendix, note xxxv.

comprehensive sketches and studies for the cartoon of it, which he prepared in Florence; and these sketches are for the greater part still in existence. This is the first work of Raphael's in which the result of his severe and profound study of Leonardo da Vinci and Michael Angelo came forth conspicuously to view, and that power of expression, that truth of attitude, and that beauty of form were manifested, which were soon to render our master so far superior to all his contemporaries and successors. Only here and there does an occasional trait, such as the gold ornaments to the garments, call to mind the earlier and youthful stage of his art. The figure of the Saviour is not dissimilar to that in Michael Angelo's group of the Pietà in St. Peter's at Rome, and, as Passavant justly points out,* it is like the figure in that piece of sculpture in its affinity with a far earlier type of the form of Christ. It has in it something of the dry and meagre style of the old school, affording, therefore, all the greater contrast with the more free and marvellous character of the two young men who are bearing the body. Quatremère de Quincy says very justly respecting this

* See Appendix, note xxxvi.

painting:* 'The man who is ascending the steps of the sepulchre backwards, exhibits the two-fold expression of moral grief and physical effort, and nothing more noble and more graceful can be conceived than the position of the young man who supports the lower part of the body. As for the grief of the Virgin and of the holy women around her, Raphael himself would have produced nothing more full of expression, had he not subsequently painted the " Bearing of the Cross," called *Lo Spasimo*.' Joseph of Arimathea, too, and the mourning John, are magnificent figures; and even in the present day we can assuredly subscribe to the words of Vasari, who, thirty years after the completion of the painting, extolled that in it which, with almost equal truth, may be asserted of it even now—that it looked as fresh as though it were only just completed.†
'And in truth,' he exclaims with enthusiasm, 'whoever contemplates the industry, the love, the art, and the grace of this work, has every cause to be astonished, as much on account of the expression in the figures as of the beauty of the drapery, and especially on account of the extraordinary excellence which is

---

* See Appendix, note xxxvii.   † See Appendix, note xxxviii.

stamped on every part.' In addition to the principal piece, Raphael painted in a smaller quadrangular compartment, a half-length figure of ' God the Father, surrounded by Angels.' This painting is still in the church of the Franciscans at Perugia; whilst the ' Theological Virtues,' with the three little angels standing between them, which was executed in grey, was taken to the picture gallery at the Vatican.

Once more our artist returned to Florence, and probably soon after he produced the magnificent half lifesize figure of St. Katharine of Alexandria, now in the National Gallery in London. The execution of this painting, which has been unsatisfactorily engraved by Desnoyers, is, it is true, slight, but it is extremely clever; the landscape background is treated as a mere sketch. Perhaps the portraits of the two youths at the Louvre belong to this epoch, but the ' Madonna' of the Tempi family certainly does; this picture was purchased by Louis . of Bavaria for 16,000 scudi, and is now in the Pinakothek at Munich.* In addition to these, he executed the beautiful life-size ' Madonna' belonging to the Niccolini family, a knee-piece painted in 1508,

* See Appendix, note xxxix.

E

now in the possession of Lord Cowper at Penshanger.
But in this painting, the expression of the Child, who
is riding on a pillow on the lap of the lovely mother,
with his left hand pushed into her bodice, is carried
to the borders of affectation—a fault which, however,
often appears at this period in Raphael—as, for example,
in the angels of the fresco painting in San Severo at
Perugia, and in the 'Madonna' of the Colonna family at
Berlin.* In addition to the two last, which belong
certainly to 1507, we might here mention also the
'Madonna with the Pink,' the original of which seems
to have been lost; the 'Madonna with the sleeping
Infant Christ,' or 'La Vierge au Linge,' at Paris, which
has been so often copied; the 'Holy Family, with the
Child on a Lamb,' at Madrid; the 'Belle Jardinière,'
in the Louvre, a painting originally executed for a
Sienese nobleman; and the 'Madonna with the Two
Children,' in the Esterhazy Gallery at Vienna.

It was about this time that Raphael became acquainted with the painter Baccio della Porta, usually
called Fra Bartolommeo, in consequence of his being a
Dominican monk of San Marco. Raphael conceived a

---

* See Appendix, note xl.

warm friendship for him, and he studied with him constantly. From him he especially learned to arrange his drapery with more magnificence, to lay on colour more broadly, and to use carmine with greater skill. How readily the young master adopted anything new which seemed to him worthy of imitation, may be seen in his unfinished 'Madonna del Baldacchino,' now in the Pitti Palace, but originally intended for the altar of the Dei family in Santo Spirito at Florence. Here we find the style of Fra Bartolommeo most faithfully imitated, so much so even, that we could have asserted that the painting was not at all the work of Raphael, but that of his friend the monk. This, however, cannot be proved with any degree of authenticity. That the picture remained unfinished was occasioned by Raphael's sudden departure for Rome in the middle of the year 1508. Pope Julius II., having already taken into his service the greatest architect of his age, Donato Lazzari of Urbino, surnamed Bramante, as well as the greatest sculptor, Michael Angelo, wished also to call his own the greatest painter of the time, and for that reason he summoned Raphael to Rome.

CHAPTER IV.

RAPHAEL IN ROME UNDER POPE JULIUS II.

1508-1513.

RAPHAEL IN ROME—EMPLOYED BY JULIUS II. TO PAINT THE APART-
MENTS OF THE VATICAN—THE SUBJECTS CHOSEN FOR THE SALA
DELLA SEGNATURA—THE 'DISPUTA DEL SACRAMENTO'—VARIOUS
OPINIONS RESPECTING THIS PAINTING—THE PRINCIPLES OF ARTISTIC
IDEALISM—'THE SCHOOL OF ATHENS'—RAPHAEL'S ADVANCE IN
PAINTING—HIS RULES OF ART—PROFESSOR BRAUN ON RAPHAEL'S
'DISPUTA'—MICHAEL ANGELO'S INFLUENCE UPON HIS ART—RAPHAEL
AND MICHAEL ANGELO—RAPHAEL'S POSITION IN ROME—LA FORNA-
RINA—RAPHAEL'S SONNETS—HIS BETROTHAL WITH THE NIECE OF
THE CARDINAL—RAPHAEL PAINTS A PORTRAIT OF HIMSELF FOR
FRANCESCO FRANCIA—RAPHAEL UNDERTAKES THE SECOND HALL OF
THE VATICAN—'THE MASS OF BOLSENA'—'THE DELIVERANCE OF
PETER'—'THE ATTILA.'

WE have seen that our artist had hitherto, in his own
advance, carefully availed himself of the experiences of
older and, indeed, of all masters, without in so doing
sacrificing and renouncing his own taste — that he
reflected these masters in his works in the most manifold manner, and theretore displayed his powers in the

most various technical changes. At first he had thrown himself with the greatest devotion into the style of the Umbrian painters, and during this period all his Madonnas, his Infant Christs, and his Saints are invested with a melancholy expression of dreamy sadness; while afterwards, when he aimed at satisfying the practical mind of the Florentines with its love of the present, he represented them in cheerful family scenes, full of the simple and healthful joys of life.* It is true, even at that time, greater things were in his soul; it is true, as Goethe says,† that he worked even then 'with ever equal and increasing ease, with a power of mind and energy maintained in due balance, with a richness of genius, giving forth the freshest water, as it were, from the first fount. Preceding masters had only conducted the youth to the threshold; he alone needed but to raise his foot to enter within the temple. Even Leonardo da Vinci and Michael Angelo, during their long life, had scarcely ever, in spite of the zenith to which their talent reached, arrived at true delight in artistic work. The one, on close examination, actually wearied himself with

* See Appendix, note xli.   † See Appendix, note xlii.

thought, and laboured too much at the technical part of his art; the other, instead of leaving behind him a multitude of sculptures in addition to those which we owe to his hand, harassed himself during the best years of his life in procuring blocks of marble from the quarries, so that after all, of all his intended heroes from the Old and New Testament, the single statue of Moses is the only thing completed which we possess, as a model of what might have been and could have been achieved.'

Even in Florence, Raphael was undeniably the greatest painter of his time; but it was not till he came to Rome that the high requirements of a bold and intellectual patron afforded that unlimited scope to the inexhaustible riches of his genius, after which he thirsted. From the provincial narrowness of a circle bounded by the taste of Urbino, Perugino, and Florence, the man, aspiring to the highest aims and standing even now at the zenith of his powers, entered a city which had been for ages the centre of civilisation, and which now especially was impelled by impulses without and within, to prove this vocation in the most important manner. To gain complete sovereignty for the apostolical see, was the restless endeavour of Julius II.

From his spiritual authority he longed to see a temporal power arise, a theocratic state κατ' ἐξοχήν; and to obtain this end, all the arts were in requisition. It was this spirit which called the cathedral of St. Peter's into life, from the ruins of a past of more than a thousand years—which raised it as a new creation, as a symbol of the spiritual power to which all other human powers were subject, partially at least realising the magnificent idea of Nicholas V., 'according to which the Vatican palace ought to be enlarged into a kind of papal city, so that not merely the Pope and his suite, but the whole body of ecclesiastics, and all spiritual officers, should find sufficient room in it, to render it truly the central point of the whole of Christendom.'* We can readily imagine what immeasurable tasks were afforded to art by such a mind —tasks, indeed, of the highest historical subjects—and how much a genius like Raphael must have been thus stimulated to open his mind to these vast historical impulses, and by this means to carry his art into a new stage of development. 'The greatness of the theme, which is the rock on which the man of weak endow-

---

* See Appendix, note xliii.

ments, unstrengthened by active mental effort, is sure
to founder,' says Ernst Guhl * with much truth, 'is to
the man of true talent, fortified by studious work, so
important a condition of his life, that nothing else can
compensate for it.' No wonder, therefore, was it that
Raphael's art reached its full maturity only. when
brought in contact with the highest demands made by
Italy at the very prime of her efforts in art and
science. From henceforth his art was no longer employed for the expression of subjective feeling, of calm
enthusiastic devotion, or for the glorification and intensity of sensuous enjoyment, but for the comprehensive idea of united humanity. After Raphael's
residence in Rome, scarcely any of his compositions
lack the dramatic interest of the action represented :
a power placing everything in motion—a great link
uniting all the characters in the painting—a spiritual
central point striking every eye—'the turn in events
—the moving action—this is almost always the soul of
the picture—it is ever one idea pervading the whole,
rendering the composition, as it were, transparently
crystal.' †

* See Appendix, note xliv.   † See Appendix, note xlv.

Raphael was called upon to decorate the state apartments. of the Vatican, and the manner in which he discharged this task gained him the name of the *philosophical* painter—a name which was only intended to denote, that he had conceived the work of the painter from that synoptic point of view which Plato ranks as the highest of human thought. The works which procured him this title were those which he executed for the Sala della Segnatura—namely, the 'Parnassus,' the 'Disputa del S. Sacramento,' the 'School of Athens,' and about fifteen smaller pictures, representing Theology, Poetry, Philosophy, and Jurisprudence.

That Raphael now and then, in the conception of these Vatican fresco paintings, applied for the assistance of the learned, appears from a letter written by him to the poet Lodovico Ariosto, in which he asks the latter about the characters to be introduced in the representation of Theology.* But, in any case, he owed the main part always to his mighty genius alone, to his intuitive tact, and to his peculiarly fine feeling ; for none of his learned friends—of those, at least, who

---

* See Appendix, note xlvi.

were especially intimate with him, such as Castiglione,
Bibbiena, and Bembo—were at that time in Rome.
We can, therefore, with reason assert, that in the
decoration of the Sala della Segnatura,* both idea and
execution are to be ascribed to Raphael alone, upon
whom the spirit of the age and the atmosphere of the
Roman *curiæ* of the day, can alone have exerted an
influence.　As a ' seasonable mark of respect in honour
of the ideas prevalent in the Vatican, from Poggio
and Salutato down to Bembo and Sadoleto'—as a
' reflection of the humanistic culture of the papal
court'—we find in this apartment ' the centre of
our spiritual existence—the foundations of moral
culture—that truth which is revealed to us as
faith, as well as that which we obtain by our own
power as knowledge—that beauty and rule of right,
the possession and enjoyment of which first stamps us
as true men—we find all these here embodied and
glorified.' †　And certainly the manner in which our
artist achieved this great and difficult task, will be
no less admired in the limitless future than it was in
the days of Pope Julius II. ; for the sight of the completed work produced such an effect on the mind of

---

* See Appendix, note xlvii.　　　† See Appendix, note xlviii.

the Pope, that he at once resolved upon having all his apartments painted by Raphael's hand.

Much which, in the 'Parnassus' and 'School of Athens,' may perhaps appear, when compared with the accuracy and strictness of style in Raphael's earlier paintings, like a certain carelessness of treatment, the partial heaviness of the figures and masses of drapery, and the occasional weakness of execution, is, however, more than counterbalanced by a sense of the beauty of the antique prevailing everywhere, the application of which to art we generally call style—by the broad, flowing, harmonious mannerism of the painting, which always increases with all painters in the same proportion as the drawing is more careless and superficial. It was in these frescoes, we may say, that Raphael first truly became the director of taste in painting ; and if Michael Angelo subsequently surpassed him in *one* point in his ceiling paintings in the Sistine Chapel— namely, in the simplification of the masses—still the former, in his elegance and just proportions, in his transitions, and in his gifted management of the brush, produced results never attainable by the latter. Indisputably, however, the most powerful lever in this new mannerism, which was calculated both to hasten for-

ward the work and to increase the general effect,
is to be perceived in the impetuous desire of an ecclesiastical prince, ardent and youthful still with regard
to mind, though physically declining, and whose undertakings extended farther and farther the nearer death
approached him.*

I must abandon all idea of a special description
of the paintings of the different apartments; it would
afford ample material for a work in itself. On the
other hand, I intend to point out briefly the various
interpretations which the 'Disputa' and the 'School of
Athens' have undergone.

Although of late, after the example of Bellori,† who
appeared in 1695 with a new interpretation, Passavant,
Trendelenburg,‡ Braun, and others, have rejected the
earlier explanations of Vasari,§ and more or less have
all given way to the modern idea that Pope Julius
intended to immortalise in painting, as two complete
contrasts, Christian theology in the 'Disputa' and
heathen philosophy in the 'School of Athens,' I feel
myself, on the other hand, fully agreed with the opinion

---

* See Appendix, note xlix.   † See Appendix, note l.
‡ See Appendix, note li.   § See Appendix, note lii.

of Herman Grimm,* that it was impossible that this supposed contrast could have been felt so keenly in the time of Julius II., and that the old interpretations of Vasàri, which were universally received for nearly two hundred years after the production of the frescoes, thoroughly correspond with the character of the age in which Julius and Raphael lived, and that, although Vasari has erred in various points, especially as regards the characters intended, on the whole he has evidently hit upon the right explanation.

Modern critics have, in the first place, greatly hesitated at the title 'Disputa del S. Sacramento;' they have called it downright nonsense, and have pointed out that Raphael himself placed over the allegorical figure of Theology, which is above the 'Disputa,' the far more explanatory inscription, 'Rerum divinarum notitia' or *Knowledge of divine things.*† Vasari, however, gives no name at all to the 'Disputa,' but only says that Raphael painted a 'Heaven with Christ and the Holy Virgin, John the Baptist, the Apostles, the Evangelists, and the Martyrs in the Clouds, with God the Father sending down His Holy Spirit upon all, and with an

---

* See Appendix, note liii.   † See Appendix, note liv.

endless number of Saints,' who are writing upon the
mass, and discussing (disputano) the different mean-
ings of the host upon the altar.   That the designation
'Disputa' was usual for such representations in Vasari's
time, is shown by Grimm from another passage of the
same author, in which he is speaking of some pictures
by living artists, arranged by a society of painters in
Florence, and among these there also appears a Disputa
of philosophy concerning the Trinity, with the heaven
opened and choirs of angels.   When, therefore, it is
asserted that it is impossible that the excitement of
the assembled multitude, so strikingly expressed in the
picture, should only proceed from such a dispute—that
something far higher is to be conveyed by it—that the
whole history of the Catholic church must be symbolically expressed by it, and in this manner the painting
is transformed into 'a theological system, the embodied
idea, as it were, of Catholicism,'—there must surely be
an error in such a verdict—an error which appears
principally to have sprung from a natural inference ; for
as the three other wall-paintings in the same apartment
represent emblematically philosophy, poetry, and jurisprudence, the 'Disputa' is naturally assigned to be the
representation of theology.   It was conjectured, as Grimm

says,[*] that 'the Pope divided the higher spiritual existence of human nature into those four parts, and wished to represent it as a whole in this apartment; and as it appeared natural that such an idea, undertaken at the command of the supreme Head of Christendom, should not be consigned for execution to the single judgment of a youthful and unlearned painter, it was imagined necessary to suppose the influence of the first spiritual authorities in Rome to have been exercised in the production of the painting.'

In accordance with this view, besides the persons who may be recognised by means of similar representations, or by the names written on the picture itself —such as popes, fathers of the church, Dante, and Savonarola—there have been discovered in the painting with more or less certainty, distinct personages, heathens, Jews, heretics, representatives of all the Christian nations of Europe, none of which were known to Vasari, or are authorised by any communication from other authors of the sixteenth or seventeenth centuries. And yet Vasari wrote his work at the direct suggestion of the circle of artistic and scientific celebrities assembled

---

[*] See Appendix, note lv.

round the young Cardinal Farnese—certainly not without profound discussions taking place as to the style and manner of the writing; and, added to this, his book passed through a second edition before his death, and in this the life of Raphael is merely furnished with a few slight additions. Although, therefore, he has doubtless erred in details—and upon this point all are agreed—we should only venture to impute to him weighty errors as regards the truth of his biography of his great contemporary, on the ground of the most convincing arguments. In what, moreover, does the ideal merit of the 'Disputa' lose, if we recognise in the picture, not a complete Catholic system of theology, not theology in the course of its scientific progress, the representation of which, moreover, transcends the limits assigned to the plastic art—but if, remaining true to Vasari's interpretation, we assume, with Springer and Grimm, that the painting depicts the moment when the clouds burst asunder, when the celestial glory of the revealed God breaks forth, rendering all further discussion useless, glorifying that visible sign of His presence, the Eucharistic feast—when, in one word, in every movement of the crowded assembly, the distinct transition from seeking to beholding truth, is evidently pour-

trayed ? * With this interpretation, what need is
there to suppose a purport still deeper, still more
significant or more learned, which would moreover not correspond with that classic idealism, the
highest representative of which in the Christian era was
undoubtedly Raphael ? ' For this true artistic idealism
is in no respect purposeless; ' it discards all material
interest as such, and embodies the whole chain of
ideas in a transparent form, beyond which and in
addition to which there is no work of art, for all is
absorbed in it.' Even in historical representations,
every outward element, and everything only outwardly
significant, disappears with this true artistic idealism ;
' it grasps alone the universally human and eternal
element, and thus releases the psychological kernel
from the historical veil that encircles it.' If, therefore,
many of the figures in the ' Disputa ' are without a name,
they are for this very reason, ' everlastingly true and
intelligible types of vague foreboding and rapturous
enthusiasm, of cautious investigation and unconditional
faith, which will be true for all times so long as the
spirit of man strives after the knowledge of the
Divine.' †

* See Appendix, note lvi.   † See Appendix, note lvii.

F

Certain it is, that the great and pervading feature of enthusiasm, uniting as it does all the persons in the painting, must always be of far more importance in its interpretation, than the explanation of the different figures connected with the history of the Church; the highest poetical beauty of the conception must ever lie in the wonderful manner in which the artist has represented the moment of surprise, the sudden effect of the glory of the opening heaven upon the most manifold individuality, yet at the same time preserving the utmost unity.

Lastly, this interpretation of the picture accords with the inscription on an old engraving of the 'Disputa,' by Giorgio Chisi, a pupil of Giulio Romano's, bearing the date of the year 1552. The purport of it is as follows :—' The principal men of the Holy Church are praising and adoring the Holy Trinity and the Majesty of God with all the inhabitants of heaven. Who ought not to be incited to piety by their example?' Upon this Grimm remarks with his nice critical judgment: *
'These words do not contradict those of Vasari's; Vasari only gives the half of the purport of the paint-

* See Appendix, note lviii.

ing; he says *what* happened, the inscription on the engraving adds *how* it happened; what with Vasari was a condition, now becomes an action. Personages of the Church entertaining different opinions upon the Trinity are interrupted in their dispute by the appearance of the Trinity itself, and by a higher power than human logic they arrive at a conclusion in which they all agree.'

Grimm has also carefully and acutely gathered together all the arguments in favour of the general justice of Vasari's interpretation of the 'School of Athens,' in contrast to that held by modern critics. Vasari says * that the picture represents ' una storia, quando i teologi accordano la filosofia e l'astrologia con la teologia.' Here, too, he again uses the word ' disputano.' The wise men of the world—Aristotle with his ethics, Plato with his Timæus † in his hand, Diogenes reclining on the steps below; to the right, the young Duke of Mantua; Raphael himself and Bramantes; Zoroaster with his globes; and among the Evangelists, St. Matthew writing, explaining the astrological figures on a board held by an angel;—these are especially pointed out by him. On

* See Appendix, note lix.   † See Appendix, note lx.

the other hand, the interpretation of Giorgio Chisi, who also engraved the 'School of Athens' in 1552, runs thus: 'Paul at Athens, brought to the Areopagus by some epicureans and stoics, standing in the midst, sees the altar with the inscription, "To the unknown God," and declares who this unknown God is. He attacks reprovingly the service of idols, counsels them to repent, and foretells the Last Judgment and the Resurrection of Christ.'

There is much in favour of this interpretation, although it is certainly striking that Vasari does not refer to it in the second edition of his work; for that he should not have known of Chisi's engraving is scarcely to be supposed. If we adhere to the idea of Plato and Aristotle, we may consider them as the representatives of two opposing sides of an old established scholastic contrast. Far more pregnantly, however, does the true interpretation stand out, as Vasari himself explains it, when we conceive the *gentile* apostle Paul represented by the side of Aristotle, that is, by the side of the Greek philosopher, who plays so great a part in the history of the Catholic theology of the scholastic age (especially since the thirteenth century, when he was made accessible to all by Latin translations and by the help of Arabic Aristotelians, such as Averrhoes), and whose metaphysics appear even in comparison with ecclesiastical dogmas as the second agent holding sway over the schools. Paul, therefore, by the side of Aristotle, signifies truly Christianity coming in contact with the old philosophy. As early as the year 1524, Agostino Venetiano, a pupil of Marc Anton's, engraved the figures of the group to the left, designated by Vasari as Evangelists; and we perceive from the writing on the pages of the book in which the Evangelist called by Vasari 'St. Matthew' is writing, that the engraving intended not him, but St. Luke. If we hold to St. Paul, this interpretation has evidently much in its favour; for, although the Greek words which Agostino placed in the book, as well as on the roll of the angel kneeling before the Evangelist, are borrowed from the gospel of St. Luke (xi. 27 and i. 42), and have no direct reference to the event here represented, relating as they do to the praise of the Holy Virgin, still St. Luke was the companion of St. Paul on the journey to Athens, and he has himself described in the Acts of the Apostles (xvii. 18) the scene which we see before us. St. Matthew was thought of probably merely because, as the only Evangelist who narrates the

journey of the wise men from the East (St. Matthew
ii. 1-12), he seemed to establish a connection with
Zoroaster and the astrologers. Modern critics, however, who will not hear of the Evangelists side by side
with the heathen philosophers, but who prefer to see
in the painting an accurate chronological history of
ancient philosophy, in opposition to that of Christian
theology in the 'Disputa,' turn St. Luke into Pythagoras,
the angel kneeling before him into his son, another
Evangelist into Heraklitus, and the man reading at the
pillar into Epicurus; and others in the same way.
But in all this there lies, in the first place, an obvious
misunderstanding of the period in which the painting
was produced; and, in the second place, the sublime
artistic idea that animates the picture loses half its
value.

At that day, as Grimm points out,* they stood on no
such high platform above things as to conceive the
Hellenic philosophy as a finished period in the mental
development of mankind. 'The works of the Greek
philosophers had in Raphael's time infused themselves
deeply into the sources of Christian learning. Plato-

* See Appendix, note lxi.

nists and Aristotelians still opposed each other as they
had done for hundreds of years; but all that had
been thought and written during these centuries
respecting this opposition, blended into a whole with
the doctrines of the two great Greeks, formed no
distinct and tangible contrast to the Christian theology,
but belonged to it so completely, that the one could
not have done without the other.' The German revolution that extended into Italy more than thirty years
afterwards, had not yet exerted its power of reaction
in the purification and limitation of Catholic Christian knowledge. Pope Julius II. was still strongly influenced even by the practical astrology of that day. Vasari,
therefore, would not have been far wrong in his union
of philosophy, astrology, and theology, even though he
may have erred in interpreting the prominent figures to
be Plato and St. Matthew, instead of St. Paul and St.
Luke. For, after all, what would be the great leading
idea of the whole representation, if Raphael had only
brought before us an array of ancient philosophers.'
What would be taking place in the picture? Whence
would arise the evident powerful emotion with which
all the personages in the painting appear seized?
What interpretation could we then assign to the

numerous figures,—children, and people of every age, who are evidently not Greek philosophers? We are ever obliged to return to Vasari's explanation, that in front to the left, the Evangelists are represented, and to the right the astrologers, while between them are the Greek philosophers, all equally occupied with the appearance of Christ, thus symbolically showing Christianity in contact with ancient philosophy and astrology; it is this interpretation alone which invests the picture with life and character. ' The astrologers have discovered that which was to prove the salvation of the world, and they have sent their tables to the Evangelists, who, translating the figures of the former into ideas and facts, write down words which fill all the bystanders with still greater joy. The composing and dissemination of the gospels, as Divine writings, depicting the manifestation of Christ, was intended to be here represented; hence, there were men and children, old and young, and even a woman among the crowd, pressing forward from the left side in the attitude of believing enquiry. And then the Greek philosophers! We see the impression which the new doctrine makes upon them also. One is absorbed in deep reflection, another is copying the writing, a third is beckoning in the distance to his friends, while the greater number remain in fixed attention. By this interpretation alone is life at once thrown into the whole mass, and their agitation and excitement is explained.' *

So much in explanation of the two principal paintings. It still remains for me to point out the immensely rapid progress made by Raphael while occupied with the pictures in the Sala della Segnatura. The 'Parnassus,' painted, indeed, on a most unfavourable portion of the wall—a window interfering with it— betrays, perhaps more than any other, more of the artist's 'graceful and somewhat meagre' Florentine style;† the figure of Apollo is a thorough failure, and the different groups appear, indeed, connected by no dramatic moment, but by outward arrangement alone; still, the separate figures are in themselves beautifully painted, and even the psychological interest is rendered conspicuous in each. There is, also, in the painting of the 'Disputa' here and there a want of true freedom, although here the somewhat antique and solemn mode of execution,

---

* See Appendix, note lxii.   † See Appendix, note lxiii.

after the example of the Florentine school of the fifteenth century, has rather an agreeable effect than otherwise. But even in this painting we perceive the trace of the greater practice he had so soon acquired; the lower part to the right required far less of subsequent touching-up with tempera colours than had been necessary before. The painting is also especially remarkable for its architectural arrangement, which is thus strikingly and briefly described by Vischer in his 'Aesthetik,' III. iii. 618 :—
'At the base, on the two sides of the altar, is a symmetrical *vis-à-vis* of fathers of the Church and laymen, having the effect of a section of a circle arched above, the ends being drawn downwards; above in the air is the solemn circle of patriarchs, apostles, and saints, this circle being arched in the reverse direction, and forming a symmetrical contrast to the lower. This segment of a circle consists, moreover, of two symmetrical halves, for it is divided in the middle by some clouds, in which—and this even is again symmetrical—four boy-angels are hovering. Above the whole appears the Saviour, with Mary and St. John at his side, and towering above all is God the Father enthroned in glory; thus forming

the pyramidal summit, the basis of which is the two circles of figures below. This apex itself also forms a symmetrical group, and above it three angels hover by the side of God the Father, but in such slight outline and delicate colouring that the pyramidal form of the top is not destroyed. The two great groups of figures, in earth and heaven, are symbolically . blended by the rays which fall from the Holy Spirit, who is represented as a dove, hovering below the figure of Christ, and which rest on the sacred elements placed on the altar. A more geometrical arrangement can scarcely be seen, and, still less so, one that triumphs so completely over stiff architectural rules, by the wonderful magnitude of the figures, by their individuality, and by the natural ease and variety of every movement.'

Christian painters and lovers of the fine arts, above all Friedrich von Schlegel,* following in their judgment the opinion of the old Lanzi,† have pronounced this painting to be the highest production of Christian art. The highest praise, however, has been awarded by Roscoe in his 'Life of Leo X.;'‡ and by many

* See Appendix, note lxiv.   † See Appendix, note lxv.
‡ See Appendix, note lxvi.

others after him, to Raphael's last work, the 'Transfiguration.' The reason for this difference of opinion
has been justly explained by the most learned interpreter of the 'Disputa,' Professor Braun, of Bonn, in
his eloquent paper 'Raphael's Disputa' (pp. 152–154),
written on occasion of the publishing of the well-
known Keller engraving. The reason he alleges is
this: that the master, standing between two periods
of art, concluded the one in the 'Disputa'—that is,
he left the naïve style, with its severe, even meagre
forms and sharp outlines, and began in the 'Transfiguration' the other style—that is, that treatment of
colour, grouping, and mode of expression, more nearly
allied to modern art. These two different schools
have, however, even to the present day (we have only
to call to mind Overbeck and Kaulbach, Schlegel and
Göthe), found their antagonistic advocates. Considered purely technically, it would be scarcely possible not to perceive a very considerable advance in
the 'School of Athens,' which, in spite of Vasari's
statement, was painted without doubt *after* the 'Disputa.' In this picture, the 'School of Athens,' one
peculiarity deserves to be noted—that this is the only
one of all Raphael's wall-paintings which is entirely

free from myth; for the master, as a true child of the Middle Ages, with their belief in miracles and marvels, never before ventured to represent historical subjects without some assisting admixture of a supernatural form, and by this means he often caused an undue interpretation, based on fable and history at the same time. This is the case, for example, in the 'Attila,' which he painted afterwards, and which we shall mention presently more particularly. Attila is induced to turn back, both by the eloquence of the Pope, and by the heavenly apparition of the two princes of the Apostles; but, as he is represented in the painting looking only to the Apostles, it is to be inferred that he is more influenced by the miracle than by the historical fact—that is, by the eloquence of the Pope.* In the 'School of Athens,' however, the artist has completely extricated his original material from that world of wonder.† Especially worthy of admiration in this painting is his management of antique costume, which he had before had no opportunity of displaying; in spite of this, he betrays in this very point a dexterity and freedom in reproducing the taste of the ancients,

* See Appendix, note lxvii.   † See Appendix, note lxviii.

such as has never been surpassed even with the far more extensive knowledge of modern artists. Besides this, the influence of Raphael's great rival, Michael Angelo, is very evident in this painting. Pope Julius II., with keen penetration, at once perceived this, and said to Sebastiano del Piombo, in 1512, 'Guardi l' opera di Rafaele, che come vidi le opere di Michelagnolo, subito lasciò la maniera del Perosino, e quanto più poteva si accostava a quella di Michelagnolo.'* (We have only to look at Raphael's works— more especially the frescoes in the Camera della Segnatura—and it becomes evident that, as soon as he had seen the paintings of Michael Angelo, he left Perugino's style, and adopted, as far as he could, that of Michael Angelo.)

Before Raphael came to Rome, he had only seen Michael Angelo's cartoon of the battle with the Pisans; he had certainly entered into no closer intimacy with him in Florence; for Michael Angelo had expressed himself contemptuously respecting both Perugino and Francia, and had therefore of course not especially attracted Raphael. The anatomical studies of Michael

* See Appendix, note lxix.

Angelo, as well as the earlier ones of Leonardo da
Vinci, had of course not been without an influence
upon the drawing of the younger master; but it was
not till he had seen the ceiling painting in the Sistine
chapel—then only half completed, the Pope having
inspected it for the first time on Christmas Day, 1512,
while the painter's scaffolding was still standing—that
he was so struck by the powerful impression, that from
that time his art experienced a complete revolution.
'Those Titan forms of Michael Angelo's, the Sybils,
produced those fairy-like genii of Raphael's, the four
beautiful female figures on the ceiling in the Stanza
della Segnatura, Poetry, Justice, Religion, and Philosophy—all of them the most exquisite types of ideal
womanhood which have ever been painted. From
the Prophets of the one, we may trace the Evangelists
in the " School of Athens " of the other—both original
works, created without the old means of exciting awe,
but full of a grand and simple truth, influencing the
mind of the observer far more deeply than any works
produced by former masters, always excepting that "Last
Supper " of Leonardo's, which, however, far away as it
was in Milan, could exert no such influence. The
" Parnassus " and the " Disputa" were executed in the

old style; the "School of Athens" is the result of his desertion of Perugino and adherence to Michael Angelo.'*

That this verdict of Grimm's has much truth in it, is not only shown by those words of Vasari,† so much commented upon and in truth so perfectly in accordance with it, 'Per le cose vedute di Michelagnolo, migliorò ed ingrandi fuor di modo la maniera e diedele più maestà,' but it is also confirmed by the whole history of Raphael's progress. To him alone was it given to learn constantly from other masters, without losing the magic sweetness of his own originality; even from his most distinct opposite, from the painter of restless passion, our artist could imitate with impunity ideal loveliness and beauty. But in what manner was this done? It was not ideas nor forms, it was not style nor grouping which Raphael borrowed from Michael Angelo, but he penetrated at once into the true mystery of a genius so opposed to his own; and while he perceived in him the quintessence of his art—that is, that which, with all his often apparent lack of artistic reflection, raised him so mightily above

* See Appendix, note lxx.   † See Appendix, note lxxi.

the commonplace and the vulgar, he did nothing but, according to Quatremère's beautiful expression, draw warmth from the flame, without in the least robbing the hearth which produced it.* Those words of Vasari's, therefore, are very far from being an undervaluing of Raphael compared with Michael Angelo; they only intend, and in this every impartial critic of the two painters must agree, that upon Michael Angelo that divine flame *first* descended from which Raphael afterwards drew light and warmth that he might attain perfection; † they in no wise contradict the further conclusion, that, if we allow that Raphael learned from Michael Angelo, we acknowledge even in this fact a decided superiority of the former to the latter, namely, in the universality of his art. If Michael Angelo towered considerably above Raphael in his free and bold independence with respect to received traditions, he lacked the capability of adding by happy imitation to his original gifts any quality in which other masters had an advantage over him; he ever remained exactly as he was, in spite of all the Raphaels round him, and not even that antique which he so highly honoured

* See Appendix, note lxxii.   † See Appendix, note lxxiii.

could he attain to in its *calm* grandeur, while Raphael, in consequence of an unequalled power appropriation, combined within himself by degre all those artistic qualities which alone in their totality constitute true art.* Vasari was certainly right in asserting that he never equalled Michael Angelo in the special art of pourtraying the naked figure; but equally true is that which this same Vasari states a little further on, namely, that out of the most different gifts of various superior masters, Raphael created a *manner of his own*, which will ever be regarded as belonging to him, and which will be held in the highest admiration.† We have here a complete acknowledgment of the universality of Raphael's art.

The little we know of the personal relation between the two masters is vague and doubtful in its value. At all events, we must not forget in examining the records that exist, that expressions of great men respecting their equals, even though they may sound severe, can never bear the significance of the trivial words of abuse with which minds of a moderate class dispute precedence with each other. Although Michael

---

* See Appendix, note lxxiv.   † See Appendix, note lxxv.

Angelo once in anger at the disputes that had occurred between him and Pope Julius II., the origin of which he imputed to the envy of Bramante and Raphael, wrote of the latter,[*] 'Whatever he knew of art, he knew through me,' there is no proof even in this bitter expression that he misjudged in the least the genius of his rival, or that he looked enviously upon him in the sense of his own weakness, and thus relapsed into a hostile feeling towards him. Herman Grimm was certainly right in drawing attention to the fact that above all things we should guard against taking the strife of partisans, and the hatred with which they may have pursued each other, as a measure of the common sentiments prevailing between two great men.[†] Among those gossiping stories, which little minds ever love to repeat of the great of the earth, we may reckon certainly the well-known anecdote of Giovanni Paolo Lomazzo,[‡] according to which Michael Angelo, one day meeting Raphael surrounded by many of his pupils, called out to him, 'There you go with your great train like a provost.' To which Raphael is said to have answered: 'And you go

* See Appendix, note lxxvi.   † See Appendix, note lxxvii.
‡ See Appendix, note lxxviii.

alone like an executioner!'* On the other hand,
there is no doubt that the amiable and much-loved
Raphael, to whom the Muses came at will, and
whose life flowed on in harmonious repose, like a
broad and clear stream, and the solitary, crabbed,
and mighty Michael Angelo, whose existence was like
some gigantic struggle, and who mastered everything
alone by contest and strife,—there is, I say, no doubt
that these two men, different as their natures were,
knew, understood, and honoured each other, even
if there was no personal feeling of love between
them.

It seems to me very significant and touching that
it was Vasari, a friend and pupil of the latter, who
was called upon to award a praise to the former,
which could alone belong to Raphael in such full
extent. He it is who drew for us a true picture of
the peculiar, nay unique, attractions of Raphael,
who first ascribed Raphael's supremacy over all
contemporary artists not so much to his masterly
power or to his worldly wisdom, but far more
to the influence of his *noble nature*. 'Among all

* See Appendix, note lxxix.

his rare gifts,' says Vasari,* 'I consider one to be so wonderful that it fills me with amazement: that, namely, with which Heaven has invested him, the power to awaken that feeling in our circle which is at variance with the nature of painters; for *all*, not only the lesser artists, but even those who claimed to be great (and art produces numbers of such), were of one mind, as soon as they worked in Raphael's presence. All ill-humour disappeared when they saw him, every low common thought was banished from the mind. Such harmony has never reigned but in the time in which he lived. And the cause was this, that they felt themselves overcome by his kindliness, by his art, and still more by the *might of his noble nature*' ('ma più dal genio della sua buona natura').

This is, though in fuller detail, just the same as Vasari so briefly and beautifully expresses at the very commencement of his biography of Raphael. His words are these: 'La Natura, quando vinta dall' arte per mano di Michelagnolo Buonarroti, volle in Raffaello esser vinta dall' arte e dei costumi insieme.' ('Nature, having been conquered by art through the hand of

---

* See Appendix, note lxxx.

Michael Angelo, was in Raphael conquered by art and manners together.')*

Whoever has had the opportunity of moving in intellectual and, at the same time, polite society, has experienced how in such a circle that man always occupies the highest place, and is involuntarily esteemed by all as the true chief, who unites with ability of no ordinary kind, a manner distinguished by delicacy of feeling and nobility of mind, the essence of true excellence, and exhibiting itself by the most unaffected and agreeable intercourse. This, however, was to be found in Raphael to the highest extent; the greatest artist was at the same time an attractive and clever man of the world, an acute judge of human nature, a man of whom Giovio in his short biography asserts with no injustice:† 'Is multa familiaritate potentium quam omnibus humanitatis officiis comparavit, non minus quam nobilitate operum, inclaruit adeo, ut nunquam illi occasio illustris defuerit ostentandæ artis.' ('He was no less famous for his friendly relations with illustrious personages, whom he knew how to place under obligations to himself, than for

* See Appendix, note lxxxi.   † See Appendix, note lxxxii.

the high order of his works, so that he never lacked a brilliant opportunity for displaying his art.')

Hence it was that even the Pope and the grandees of the Roman court solicited Raphael's friendship, that he lived in Rome in wealth and luxury, as no artist had done before him, that, when he went to the Vatican, 'cinquanta pittori tutti valenti e buoni' accompanied him in solemn procession, bearing witness before everyone how truly they felt they were honouring themselves in showing him the highest honour, so that Vasari might justly write of him : 'Egli in somma non visse da pittore ma da principe.' * One alone, the great Michael Angelo, stood gloomily and unsociably aside, tendering no homage to him, pursuing his high aim alone along steep and giddy paths, while Ascanio Condivi in his 'Vita di Michelangelo Buonarotti' (Rome, 1553) places this beautiful expression in the lips of Raphael : 'I esteem myself happy to have been born in the times of Michael Angelo, for through him I have learned another art than that of the old masters.'

'Like Achilles and Hercules,' says Grimm,† 'the

* See Appendix, note lxxxiii.   † See Appendix, note lxxxiv.

two great men stand side by side, like vigorous beauty
shedding its light on all around, contrasted with
gloomy power overcoming everything in its might, or,
like a short and sunny spring contrasted with a
long year, beginning in tempest, and amid tempest
ceasing.' But as regards the dispute continued even
up to the present day, as to which of the two merits
precedence as an *artist*, Raphael or Michael Angelo,
we can only answer in the words of Göthe: 'It is
difficult to comprehend one great talent alone, let us
say nothing, therefore, of two at once. We lighten the
task by partiality, hence the estimation in which
artists and authors are held always fluctuates, and one
or the other exclusively rules the day. Such disputes
have not perplexed me, because I have always let them
alone, and occupied myself with more immediate
examination of all that is valuable and estimable.' *
And in another passage in his ' Italienischen Reise,' he
writes similarly: 'Now it was Raphael, now it was
Michael Angelo, who held precedence, a fact from which
this only could be drawn at last: that man was such a
limited being that, if his mind did open to greatness,

* See Appendix, note lxxxv.

he never attained a capacity for equally estimating and acknowledging greatness of different kinds.' *

It is certain that in the time in which Raphael lived, it was not he, but Michael Angelo, who was regarded as the greatest artist, nay, even between the two, Leonardo da Vinci was for a time placed, and only a third rank was awarded to the painter of the beautiful. 'Tertium in pictura locum Raphael Urbinus mira docilis ingenii suavitate atque solertia adeptus est' ('the third place in painting belongs to Raphael d'Urbino, from the wonderful sweetness and versatility of his well-disciplined mind '), says Paolo Giovio; and even in Vasari's biography, in spite of all his admiration of the fascinating nature of the artist, there is a certain coolness in his critical examination of his works, which evidently does not proceed merely from a one-sided preference for Michael Angelo, but faithfully reflects the tone of feeling of the public of the day. Why Passavant, however, should, on the other hand, grow so warm, and should take Giovio especially to task, because he allows us to see that Raphael owed his great distinction principally to his

* See Appendix, note lxxxvi.

versatile powers, is not easily conceivable;* we should far rather be astonished had it been otherwise. Mozart, too, was in his own day never acknowledged as the first master of melody, and it is just this circumstance which raises Raphael's everlasting fame above all attack, that his contemporaries even then, although they had not yet penetrated to the full merit of the artist, still with one voice extolled to the uttermost the divine harmony existing between his nature and his art. Happy is the master whose character is estimated by admiring contemporaries no less than his works. He need have no care for his after-fame; for it is not merely what the man has done, but what he has been, that passes on to generations to come, and it is only then, when being and doing are but one, that our highest greatness and imperishable fame are to be attained.

Soon after Raphael's arrival in Rome, he appears to have formed an affection which only terminated with his death, though it cannot be considered quite certain whether it was always one and the same maiden whom he loved during this period. According to the records

* See Appendix, note lxxxvii.

of the Abbate Melchior Missirini, which are, moreover, not very credible, his beloved was the daughter of a turf-burner, living near Santa Cecilia, on the other side of the Tiber.* A small house ornamented with a beautiful antique window-frame is still pointed out in the Contrada Santa Dorotea, No. 20, as her birth-place. From the annotated copy, of the sixteenth century, of the second Florentine edition of Giorgio Vasari's biographies of the year 1568, now in the possession of the advocate Giuseppe Bannutelli in Rome (fol. 78), it appears, according to Passavant,† that the girl was called Margarita ; she is now generally called the Fornarina, without any direct testimony whence the name arose. She may have been the same maiden who, according to Vasari, was in Raphael's house at the time of his death, and upon whom he settled a comfortable maintenance in his will, but suppositions of this kind belong rather to the treasures of fable than of truth.‡

Certain it is, that ever the same female figure appears in many of Raphael's studies and sketches ; also a portrait painted by him in oils may lay decided

* See Appendix, note lxxxviii. † See Appendix, note lxxxix.
‡ See Appendix, note xc.

claim to be a likeness of his beloved, even if not of her whom we designate the Fornarina. This picture, probably belonging to an earlier period, is now in the Barberini Palace in Rome; it represents a young maiden, not completely dressed, having only shortly before left her bath; she is sitting in a grove of myrtles and laurel-trees, her head encircled with a turbanlike yellow-striped handkerchief; her right hand presses a transparent linen garment to her bosom, while her lap, on which her left hand rests, is covered with red drapery. Her left arm is adorned with a gold bracelet, and on this Raphael has written his own name. Herman Grimm speaks of another picture, which might possibly represent this youthful being in maturer years; [*] formerly in the possession of Kestner, the counsellor of the embassy in Rome, and unfortunately much injured and defaced: it is now in the gallery belonging to his heirs in Hanover. As in the youthful figure in the Barberini Palace, we see here also a handkerchief wound round her head; we seem to have the same hair before us, the same delicate throat, only everything is more refined, more mature, more

---

[*] See Appendix, note xci.

spiritual. Her hands are grasping a fur cloak, which is thrown over her shoulders, and is falling off, leaving bare her bosom, which is covered with a low-drawn finely folded garment, and in the middle, just where the garment is fastened with a knot, and slightly parts, there falls a golden chain. Thus Grimm describes the portrait, which I myself saw in Rome in Kestner's possession in 1852.

That Passavant should recognise in a picture existing in the Pitti Palace since 1824—a picture which probably owes the honour of being called an original of Raphael's, only to the circumstance that something in the expression of the countenance reminds of the 'Sistine Madonna'—that Passavant should recognise in this picture the naïve fresh child of nature developed into a proud Roman lady with a powerful frame and royal demeanour, and should perceive in this painting, therefore, a second genuine portrait of the so called Fornarina, is to me perfectly inconceivable, as it seems to me, and equally so to Grimm, to have a thoroughly different expression and cast of countenance.* Passavant himself considers it not entirely

* See Appendix, note xcii.

painted by Raphael's own hand; the head is executed
with much spirit, the linen drapery covering the bosom,
and the full damask sleeve, are masterly, but the other
parts of the picture appear to him less finished in style.*

On the other hand, I will not dispute that much
that reminds us of this portrait is to be found in
many of Raphael's female figures, for instance in the
large 'Holy Family' at the Louvre, in the figures of
the frescoes for the story of Psyche in the Farnesina,
and even, although thoroughly idealised, in the 'Sistine
Madonna;' and equally little will I contest the further
statement of Passavant's as to the existence of an
engraving of Marc Anton's from a slight sketch of
Raphael's, in which his beloved one is represented at
the very moment that she is sitting to him for a picture of a Madonna, contemplating herself pleasantly in a
small mirror, in which a man, standing behind her, and
bearing every appearance of a portrait, is also looking.
This may be her servant Baviera. But whether the
'una sua Donna,'†—who, according to Vasari,‡ at
one time so completely drew away the master from his
work, that his friend Chigi at length could devise no

---

* See Appendix, note xciii.   † See Appendix, note cxiv.
‡ See Appendix, note cxv.

other means than to bring the beautiful woman to him
on his painter's scaffold, where she sat the whole day
by his side, and he could carry on his work without
being deprived of her company—whether this charmer
was identical with the so called Fornarina, and whether
the four sonnets which were written in Raphael's handwriting on the back of some studies for the wall
painting of the ' Disputa,' and which are still in preservation, were addressed to this same beloved one or to
some other, is not at all certain. So far alone we can
safely assert that these ardent poems were written
during the artist's residence in Rome (probably in
1508), and that he finished them off with great care,
in spite of the overwhelming passion to which they
certainly owe their origin. And I confess that this
latter circumstance is to me far more interesting than
all the investigations for details of Raphael's amours;
for they excite the imagination tenfold on account of
the very obscurity in which they are wrapped. We
perceive again, moreover, from this fact that the
master ever endeavoured to make everything which he
undertook as perfect as possible, and we thus gain a
valuable addition to the completion of that portrait of
his noble character which it is our object to delineate.

I will here insert these valuable poetical effusions in
their due order :—

1.

Un pensier dolce è rimembrare il modo
    Di quello assalto, ma più grave il danno
    Del partir, ch' io restai come quei ch' hanno
    In mar perso la stella, se 'l ver odo.
Or lingua di parlar dissogli il nodo,
    A dir di questo inusitato inganno
    Ch' amor mi fece per mio grave affanno,
    Ma lui pur ne ringrazio, e lei ne lodo.
L' ora sesta era che l' occaso un sole
    Aveva fatto, e l' altro surse in loco,
    Atto più da far fatti che parole.
Ma io restai pur vinto al mio gran foco
    Che mi tormenta, chè dove l' uom sole
    Disiar di parlar, più riman fioco.

(The original is at Oxford.)

'Tis sweet in thought to embrace thee once again !
    But waking from my dream, thy loss comes back ;
    And like some mariner who has lost his track,
    And finds a starless heaven, I remain.
Let my tongue burst its fetters, and disclose
    How Love destroyed me with his cunning ways,
    And drew me down to my own loss and woes;
    But yet I thank his wiles, and her I praise.
'Twas even, and one sun had long declined,
    When in its place that other sun arose
    With speechless action, utterance to find.

Thus have I been by cruel thoughts assailed
   With their tormenting power; for when I pined
   To vent my grief in words, all utterance failed.

II.

Amor, tu m' invescasti con due lumi
   Dei occhi dov' io me strugo, e face
   Da bianca neve e da rose vivace,
   Da un bel parlar, e d' onesti costumi.
Tal che tanto ardo che nè mar nè fiume
   Spegner potrian quel foco, ma piace
   Poich' il mio ardor tanto di ben mi face
   Ch' ardendo ognor più d' arder mi consuma.
Quanto fu dolce al giogo! E la catena
   De' suoi candidi bracci al col mio volti
   Che scegliendomi io sento mortal pena.
D' altre cose non dico che son molti,
   Chè soverchia dolcezza a morte mena,
   E però taccio, a te i pensier rivolti.

(Oxford.)

Love, that ensnar'st me with thy magic light
   From eyes that melt me into hope and fears;
   Like snow on roses lying she appears
   With word and actions to inspire delight.
Until so warm my flame, that no sea wave
   Could quench the burning ardour that I know;
   Yet revelling in the flame I feel its glow,
   Nor wish from its consuming power to save.

H

How sweetly passive was she when controll'd;
　Throwing her white arms as a chain around,
　Until it seemed like death to loose their hold.
Yet pause I here, tho' still my thoughts abound;
　For joys excessive, fatal powers enfold;
　Yet while I cease, to thee my thoughts are bound.

III.

Come non potè dir arcana Dei
　Paul, quando disceso fù dal cielo,
　Così il mio cor d' uno amoroso velo
A ricoperto tutti i pensier miei.
Però, quanto ch' io viddi e quanto fei
　Pel gaudio taccio che nel petto celo,
　E prima cangerò nel fronte il pelo
Che mai l' obbligo volga i pensier rei.
Guarda al ardor mio, non abbi appico,
　Che, send' io tuo soggetto, mi or concede
　Che per mia fiamma ardresti apoco, apoco.
E se 'l pregarmi in te avesse loco,
　Giammai non restaria chiamar mercede
　Sin che nel petto fosse il parlar fico.

　　　　　　　　　　　　　　　(*Oxford.*)

As Paul from mortal ear those words withheld
　Which he had heard in Paradise above,
　So round my heart is drawn a veil of love,
　By which my thoughts in secrecy are held.
Hence all I did and all that sight revealed,
　From my own bosom none shall dare to know;
　And my dark locks to silvery white shall grow,
　Ere night shall open all that lies concealed.

. Yet see my passion, and vouchsafe this grace,
    That being thine, it may be granted me,
    That thou wouldst burn a little for my flame;
And if my prayers with thee may find a place,
    Ne'er would I pause thy piteous help to claim
    Until the powers of utterance silent be.

Of the fourth sonnet there exist only the two first verses, and these are in some parts doubtful, as Raphael's manuscript, now in the Musée Favre at Montpellier, is very carelessly and illegibly written:—

IV.

Fello pensier, ch' in te cercar affanni
    E dare in preda il cor per più sua pace,
    Or vedi tu gli effetti aspri e tenace
    Sciolti che m' usurpar i più belli anni.
Ma le fatiche, e voi, famosi affanni,
    Risvegliate il pensier che in ozio giace,
    Mostrategli quel colle alto che face
    Salir dai bassi ai più sublimi scanni.

Sad thought! that unto thee I gave my heart,
    Seeking for peace, and finding nought but pain;
    Seest thou the bitter anguish and the smart
    . With which life's fairest years are from me ta'en?
But ye, my efforts, and thou, aching grief,
    Waken the thought that had in slumber lain,
    And point to paths, ascending which I gain
    Sublimer heights that may afford relief.

Here the sonnet breaks off; but with all its deep
anguish of love it exhibits also a strong manly feeling
of genuine genius, endeavouring to regain compo-
sure by a return to artistic work. On account of this
moral turn, this fragment appears to me almost more
important and characteristic than the other more
perfect poems.

Raphael was never married. In a letter to his uncle
Simone Ciarla, dated July 1, 1514, he touches upon
the subject in a business-like manner, and says, far
from all sentimentality, that he had refused in Rome
very different persons to those now proposed to him in
his native city Urbino; that he did not wish to enter
into any proposals of marriage, nor did he desire a
wife, that he had never got so far with anyone
where he now was, and he thanked God daily for
having acted so wisely. Nevertheless he did not refuse
the hand of the young Maria di Bibbiena, the niece of
the Cardinal Santa Maria in Portico,* who was just at
that time proposed to him. Still, however, he postponed
the marriage, according to Vasari, because he hoped to
be appointed Cardinal—an appointment which, when we

---

* See Appendix, note xcvi.

consider the Roman affairs of that period, is in itself not so utterly incredible as the interpreters of Vasari imagine;* for Leo X. appointed a number of cardinals, principally for the sake of the large sums which by this means flowed into his coffers. And Raphael himself was rich·; he was a favourite with the Pope, and, as Grimm alleges, he was a kind of chief minister in the Fine Arts, which were all-important in the eyes of Leo X. That, as some maintain, the alliance with the niece of the Cardinal was prevented by her death, which took place shortly before his own, is by no means a settled matter. The well-known difficult passage in the above-mentioned letter, 'Siamo più che mai alle strette,' may be translated as by Grimm, 'We (that is, the Cardinal and I) are on the point of breaking off the affair;' or it may be translated as by Guhl and Passavant, 'We are more than ever approaching the conclusion.' With regard to what follows, when Raphael consoles his uncle, and begs him to wait for the moment when he and Bibbiena should have come to an explanation, and that, in case the affair should be put an end to, he would submit to the wish of his

---

* See Appendix, note xcvii.

uncle, I must give the preference to Grimm's interpretation.* Even though, according to his own last
will, the remains of Maria, as his betrothed, were to
be placed by the side of his own in the same chapel of
the Pantheon—and that this was done is evidenced by
the inscription found there †—even this affords no proof
against Grimm's interpretation, for the betrothal could
very reasonably have taken place in 1514, not long
before the breach, without having been in consequence
ever wholly given up; and we can well imagine that
Raphael, out of consideration for Bibbiena, willingly
allowed that Maria's name should come before posterity as that of his affianced, although he had for a
long time given up the idea of a union with her. At
the same time it may be left undecided whether there
is any truth or no in the supposition of Vasari's editor,
that she was 'malaticcia' (sickly), and that this circumstance favoured the postponement of the marriage,
according to Raphael's desire.

We must now take up the threads of our narrative
after this lengthy digression. In a letter of September 5, 1508, published by Count Malvasia in his

---

* See Appendix, note xcviii.   † See Appendix, note xcix.

'Felsina Pittrice,' ii. 48, Raphael promised his friend
Francesco Francia in Florence a portrait of himself in
return for that of Francesco. 'I must beg you,'
writes Raphael, 'to make allowance for me, and to
pardon my delay and postponement in sending you my
own (that is, my portrait) which, from my unin-
terrupted and important occupations, I have not as
yet been able to finish, according to our agreement. I
might certainly have sent you one, executed by one of
my pupils and retouched by myself, but that would not
have been right. I will at once set about the task,
though the result will not equal the merit of your
work.'* It is probable that, in consequence of this
promise, that knee-piece was executed in which Raphael, with his face at three quarters, is represented
sitting at a table covered with a cloth, on which his
right arm rests, his hand falling over it, while his left
hand holds his fur-bordered cloak. Prince Adam Czar-
toryski purchased the picture in Venice in 1807; at
1850 it was brought from St. Petersburg to England,
and was engraved by Paul Pontius. A copy of it is
at Stuttgart. At the same time another painting of

---

* See Appendix, note c.

Raphael's, an 'Annunciation,' was sent to Bologna, but all further information respecting it is lost; a copy of it, however, is to be seen in the castle at Gotha. It is probable that Francia wrote his well-known sonnet, that touching proof of his high esteem for a friend so much his junior in years, on the arrival of this picture. The superscription is as follows: 'To the excellent painter Raphael Santi, the Zeuxis of our age, from me Francesco Raibolini, surnamed Francia.' We will insert the poem :—

> Non son Xeusi ne Apelle, e non son tale
>   Che di tanti tal nome a me convegna,
>   Ne mio talento, ne vertùde è degna
>   Haver da un Raffael lode immortale.
> Tu sol, cui fece il ciel dono fatale
>   Che ogn' altro eccede, e fora ogn' altro regna,
>   L' eccellente artificio a noi insegna
>   Con cui sei reso ad ogn' antico uguale.
> Fortunato garzon, che nei primi anni
>   Tant oltrepassi, e che sarà poi quando
>   In più provecta etade opre migliori?
> Vinta sarà natura ; e da tuoi inganni
>   Resa eloquente dirà te lodando
>   Che tu solo il pictor sei da' pictori.

> Nor Zeuxis' nor Apelles' art is mine,
>   That such high honours I should dare to claim;
>   Nor am I worthy of the immortal fame
>   A Raphael to my talent would assign.

Such gifts has Providence on thee alone
. Bestowed, choice gifts of long-enduring fame;
Thou teachest men true art, making thy name
Equal with ancient painters in renown.
Oh happy youth! if thou dost so excel
When but a few short summers thou hast known,
What wilt thou be when ripe with studious years?
Then will thy magic hand its victories tell,
And vanquished nature ring thy praise alone,
That amid painters thou hast no compeers.

During the first three years of his residence in Rome, Raphael painted the long-lost but often-copied 'Madonna di Loretto' for the church of Santa Maria del Popolo, which was brought from Florence by Sir Walter Kennedy Laurie in June 1857, and exhibited before the Accademia di San Luca in Rome, who pronounced it to be genuine.* He painted also for the same church the splendid portrait of Julius II., which is now in the Pitti Palace; the portrait of the young marquis Federigo di Mantova, now in England; † and that of Parmesano, a favourite of the Pope's, a painting which was found in Rome a few years ago by a printseller named Valati, and sold to an Englishman.‡ He

* See Appendix, note ci. † See Appendix, note cii.
‡ See Appendix, note ciii.

also executed the 'Madonna of the House of Alba' for the church of the Olivetans at Nocera de' Pagani in the kingdom of Naples: this painting is now in the Hermitage at St. Petersburg. The 'Madonna with the Diadem' ('Vierge au Diadème,' or, as Desnoyers calls it, 'Vierge au Linge') in the Louvre, and the 'Madonna of the Aldobrandini family,' in the possession of Lord Garvagh in London, also belong to this period, as well as the great 'Madonna di Fuligno,' painted about the year 1511, as an altar-piece for Sigismondo Conti of Fuligno, the Pope's private secretary. This picture was formerly in the church of Araceli, but it is now in the Vatican. This painting is especially remarkable for that deeper golden tint which was never apparent in the earlier works of the master, as well as for the chiaroscuro in the charming boy-angel who holds the tablet—one of the most exquisite forms ever painted by Raphael. It reminds us somewhat of the manner of Sebastiano del Piombo, who was at that time making a great noise in Rome.

In the year 1512, by order of the German nobleman Johannes Gorizius of Luzembourg, the master painted the 'Prophet Isaiah' al fresco on one of the pillars of the church of St. Augustine in Rome. This picture, which has

more of Michael Angelo's manner in it than any other
work of Raphael's—perhaps just for the very reason
that he endeavoured in this painting to lay aside his
own individuality—holds an inferior place among his
other works, in spite of the remarkable correctness of
the drawing.   The figure is somewhat clumsy, and
there is a want of expression in the countenance ; besides, though restored by Daniele da Volterra, it is now
much destroyed.   That even at that time the painting
did not afford full satisfaction is evidenced by the
following circumstance : Raphael demanded fifty scudi
for it ; the price was, however, considered too high, and
the execution of the other frescoes in the church was
not conferred upon him.*   Among the other pictures
belonging to this same period is the portrait of a lady
in the Tribune at Florence, in which sometimes the
Fornarina has been endeavoured to be recognised,
sometimes Vittoria Colonna, sometimes the Duchess Elizabeth of Urbino, and sometimes Beatrice d'Este, the
wife of Lodovico Sforza.   Passavant,† however, gives
plausible reasons for considering the picture to be a
certain Beatrice Pio of Ferrara.   There are also a por-

* See Appendix, note civ.   † See Appendix, note cv.

trait of Bindo Altoviti, a Florentine youth, twenty-two years of age, with fair hair and blue eyes, now in the Pinakothek at Munich;* and the 'Madonna dell' Impannata' (so called- from the window in the background, covered with a sort of linen curtain): this picture, however, is not entirely the work of Raphael's own hand, and may even perhaps have been executed later; it is now in the Pitti Palace. Besides these, there are the 'Madonna dell' Passeggio,' in the Bridgewater Gallery in London; the 'Madonna with the Standing Child,' in the possession of Mr. Mackintosh in England (called the 'Madonna della Torre'†): this picture also probably left the atelier of the master without any special part in its production having been taken by himself. And, lastly, there are the 'Holy Family' in Naples, painted for Leonello da Carpi, Lord of Meldola; and the 'Madonna del Pesce, with the Archangel Raphael, St. Jerome, and the young Tobit,' who is holding a fish. This painting is now in the Museum at Madrid, and is a large altar-picture; it was engraved by Steinla in 1856, in large folio size. From the power and repose of its colouring, it is most

---

* See Appendix, note cvi.   † See Appendix, note cvii.

effective even at the present day, although it has in some parts suffered by having been transferred from wood to canvas by Bonnemaison in Paris, and it has moreover been retouched by no skilful hand.*

Raphael next proceeded in the decoration of the second hall of the Vatican, which, from the principal painting in it, is called La Stanza d' Eliodoro. In this hall is depicted the divine protection which the church enjoys, as well as its safety from dangers without and within. During the lifetime of Pope Julius IL, however, who died in 1513, the master only completed the 'Expulsion of Heliodorus from the Temple,' and the 'Miracle of Bolsena.' In the year 1514, these were followed by two wall paintings, the 'March of Attila' and the 'Deliverance of Peter from Prison;' by four ceiling paintings, 'God appearing to Noah,' 'Abraham's Sacrifice,' 'Jacob's Dream of the Heavenly Ladder,' and 'God appearing to Moses in the Burning Bush;' and by twelve·allegorical figures and four Hermæ, serving as Caryatidæ and socle-pictures under the wall frescoes. Lastly, he executed six small pictures in the window recesses, some of which are now quite unknown, or have

* See Appendix, note cviii.

been newly painted. These were, 'Joseph before Pharaoh,' 'The Red Sea,' 'Moses receiving the Tables of the Law,' 'The Annunciation,' 'A Pope celebrating Mass, and surrounded by Four Ecclesiastics,' and the 'Emperor Constantine giving up the City of Rome to Pope Sylvester.' Raphael received 1,200 ducats in gold for all these works together. The gold ducat or 'fiorino' had, according to the standard of 1269, a value of 711½ grains of fine silver; it was therefore equal to five shillings and sevenpence of our money. According to this, our artist therefore received 335*l*.*

The most distinguished of all the pictures we have named is indisputably the 'Mass of Bolsena,' in which Raphael represented 'the miraculous assistance of God to His church in confuting the unbelievers in the sacred mysteries;' while in 'Heliodorus' he intended to exhibit 'the divine protection vouchsafed to the church in her outward relations.'† In the year 1263, in the time of Pope Urban IV., a priest, doubting the miracle of transubstantiation, was, according to tradition, brought back to the faith in the church of Sta. Cristina at Bolsena, by the miraculous

* See Appendix, note cix.   † See Appendix, note cx.

flowing of blood from the Host, as he was himself celebrating Mass. This story forms the subject of the first-mentioned painting, the colouring of which is well preserved, and, though almost ten years before the Venetian school reached its prime, it displays all the technical superiority of that style. All that which we admire in Titian's works—' the overwhelming power and warmth of his tints, the tender subordinate feeling of his transitions, his half tints, and his blending of colours, with all his rich energetic manner,'—all this is to be found in its highest perfection in this incomparable painting.* The design and conception of the whole equals the beauty of the colouring. Rumohr was right when he asserted that the two levers of the political affairs of Europe at the beginning of the sixteenth century—namely, the priesthood and the German soldiery—have been nowhere so clearly and objectively represented as here. The upper group in the picture exhibits Julius II. with some of his cardinals and pliable spiritual courtiers—affording a strong contrast to the German bluntness and honest stubbornness displayed in the figures of the Swiss guards.

* See Appendix, note cxi

The 'Heliodorus' is rather more carelessly executed;
but still, in this painting also, we see in some portions
the original colouring in all its power and freshness.
In its subject, the work is in nowise inferior to the
'Mass of Bolsena;' and for this reason it is especially
worthy of observation, that in this painting Raphael
first represented, after the manner of Michael Angelo
and Leonardo da Vinci, not only figures in rest or in
calm action, but also the violent and rapid movements
of both men and animals.   Dramatic passion, which the
earlier painters never thought of producing, is expressed
even here with most masterly power; and this is a fresh
proof how rapidly Raphael's genius grasped every new
theme and fitted itself for its execution.

In the picture of the 'Deliverance of Peter' it is
especially the distribution of light and shade which
makes it so effective.   The whole may be divided into
three parts.   In the two first, Raphael makes the light
proceed from the supernatural lustre of the Angel who
is liberating the Apostle, while in the third, the light
comes from the torch held by one of the watchmen, and
from the moon in the cloudy heaven.

The execution of the 'Attila' is also very masterly.
The figures of the Apostles Peter and Paul are espe-

cially life-like in outline and brilliant in colour; they appear with drawn swords on the left side of the picture, above the Pope, who is riding along calmly and solemnly on a grey horse. Most effective, too, are the countenances in the papal train, all of which are portraits, and in contrast to these we see Attila with his hordes, as well as two men riding on wild horses, to the right in the foreground; still the horses appear some-what too clumsy and thick—after Raphael's manner,* who, in this respect, certainly never reached the highest stage of perfection—though the peculiarity in the breed of Roman horses, even at the present day, may afford in some measure an excuse or explanation for this. The historical part of the picture is as follows:—'The great Bishop of Rome, Leo I., was in the year 452 marching forward with negotiations of peace to meet the all-conquering King of the Huns, who was approach-ing Rome. On the banks of the Oglio, near the fortress of Governolo, he met Attila, and presented him with gifts, according to the custom of the time, in couse-quence of which he retreated; a subsequent legend, however, represented this retreat of Attila as caused by

* See Appendix, note cxii.

I

the miraculous interference of the Apostle Peter. As the long-desired expulsion of the French from Italy took place at the time of the origin of the painting, Pope Leo X. having succeeded, with the help of the Swiss, in overcoming Louis XII. in 1513, Raphael represented Leo X. in the figure of the Pope.

The socle pictures, lastly, were flattering allusions to the rule of this Pope. They represented 'Religion,' 'Law,' 'Peace,' 'Protection,' 'Nobility,' 'Commerce,' 'Naval Affairs,' 'Navigation,' 'Plenty,' 'Cattle-breeding,' 'Agriculture,' and 'Grape-gathering.' According to their Italian denominations, they were all female figures, which, painted in grey and gold, have become much injured. Some of them were completely renovated by Carlo Maratti and his pupils, in the years 1702 and 1703.

CHAPTER V.

RAPHAEL UNDER LEO X.

1513–1520.

JULIUS II. AND LEO X.—THE LOGGIE—THE CARTOONS—RAPHAEL DECORATES THE STANZA DELL' INCENDIO—THE SALA DI COSTANTINO —THE SALA DE' PALAFRENIERI—THE INFLUENCES SURROUNDING RAPHAEL—THE COURT OF LEO X.—RAPHAEL'S PORTRAITS—THE PROPHETS AND SIBYLS—THE GALATEA—RAPHAEL'S VIEWS OF ART— RAPHAEL'S ARCHITECTURAL WORKS—APPOINTED ARCHITECT OF ST. PETER'S—HIS DESIGN FOR THE COURT OF THE VATICAN—PASSAVANT'S OPINION OF HIS ARCHITECTURAL SKILL—THE UNIVERSALITY OF HIS GENIUS—THE MADONNA DELLA SEDIA—LO SPASIMO DI SICILIA— THE MADONNA DI SAN SISTO—THE TRANSFIGURATION—RAPHAEL'S ILLNESS AND DEATH.

IT is to Pope Julius II. that art owes the determination to call forth the youthful and fertile genius of Raphael into fuller development, by the commission to adorn the halls of the Vatican with great historical pictures; for, without such a commission, it is probable that, in the short career of the artist, he would have entered upon nothing, or at least upon nothing of the same magnitude. This energetic Mæcenas, therefore, in the course of a pontificate of scarcely ten years—that is, from October 18, 1503, to February 15, 1513—led the art of the *two* greatest masters of his time (for we must here again call to mind Michael Angelo's Sistine Chapel) to that unattained height to which all after generations have looked up with devout amazement, without ever being able to produce anything similar. It is true the Pope possessed but little learning, yet his love of genius and his energy of will compensated for this, and, as Rumohr beautifully remarks,* inspired him, in his intercourse with two great men, with foresight of the achievements of which their talent was capable, with the belief in possibility of what was still untried, with courage for great undertakings, and, lastly, with the power to guard against the divisions which deprive weak characters of the means of greatness.

Julius's successor, Leo X., on the contrary, who as a patron of art is ever ranked far higher by the historian of letters than he rightly deserves, was certainly a highly cultivated ecclesiastical prince, but,

* See Appendix, note cxiii.

unlike his predecessor, he was neither a politician, nor was he distinguished for nobility of character. In the midst of learned researches and art, he was often delighted with the most empty and even obscene pastimes. The 'Notizie inedite di Raffaello da Urbino,' only lately discovered by the Marchese Giuseppe Campori in the archives of the Este family in Modena,* and there published, tell us that the tossing of monks in a blanket, and the foot-races of naked men, were occasionally the diversions of the Pope. The narrow interests of his house—he was, as all the world knows, a Medicean—a certain luxurious free-thinking character, the inertia of a pleasure-loving mind of no great depth, but with ready powers of comprehension, and a trifling superficial participation in every possible matter—all these took precedence of the true duties of his office; he wasted his colossal resources in his immoderate love of ostentation, and all his artistic undertakings lacked, in consequence, grandness of design and energy of execution. Thus it was that, while Julius II. had exclusively occupied Raphael's time and creative power, Leo X., with all his high personal

---

* See Appendix, note cxiv.

esteem and admiring friendship, left him full leisure
to bestow his best powers on subordinate work for
distant churches and wealthy citizens. After the completion of the Stanza d' Eliodoro, in which the mind
of Julius II. was fully carried out, Raphael painted
for the new Pope, during a period of more than seven
years, nothing but the sketches for the Loggie, a
number of cartoons on canvas, the frescoes in the
Stanza dell' Incendio (these latter, however, only
partially), two designs for the Sala di Costantino, and
little else; whilst, within five years, he had executed
for Julius II. far more and far greater works.

The Loggie are in the vestibule which opens towards
the courtyard, and leads, in the second story of the
Vatican, from the staircase to the apartments, consist-
ing of thirteen dome-like divisions. These contain
forty-eight representations from the Old, and four from
the New Testament, all of the highest antique beauty,
and, besides these, arabesque ornaments on the walls
and pillars, exhibiting the richest and most playful
fancy; and, lastly, twelve pictures, as if in relief, of a
golden brown metallic colour, in the socle below the
windows, the small sketches for which Raphael himself
drew out in sepia, giving up the execution in fresco to

his pupils Francesco Penni, Pellegrino da .Modena, Polidoro da Caravaggio, Perino del Vaga, Giovanni da Udine, and others, under the direction of Giulio Romano. We have some striking remarks of Göthe upon these Loggie in his paper, 'Von Arabesken,' though in his 'Italienische Reise' he asserts, with a certain avowed partiality,* that these ingenious trifles ought not to be looked at after the great figures of Michael Angelo's fresco paintings in the Sistine Chapel, and that these biblical stories, beautiful as they are, cannot stand the test of those.† In the first-mentioned passage, however, the poet, comparing the arabesques of the Loggie with similar productions by the ancients, thus expresses himself:—' Those famous arabesques with which Raphael decorated a part of the Loggie of the Vatican are indeed beautiful in another sense; it is as if he had wished to show lavishly what he could devise, and what the skilful workmen who surrounded him could execute. There is therefore here none of that wise parsimony of the ancients, who only endeavoured, as it were, to complete one building, that they might be able to enjoy it; but here is an artist who

* See Appendix, note cxv.   † See Appendix, note cxvi.

worked for the sovereign of the world, and who desired as much as his master did to erect a monument of profuse abundance.'

From 1515 to 1516, Raphael worked, with the assistance of Francesco Penni and Giovanni da Udine, at the coloured cartoons for the ten tapestries to be executed at Arras in wool, silk, and gold.* These tapestries were originally intended for the lower wall of the Sistine Chapel, but since 1814, after various wanderings, they have been removed to the upper apartment of the Vatican. They represent ten events in the history of the Apostles. Only seven, however, of these cartoons are at present in existence, and these are in the palace at Hampton Court.† Their subjects are—the 'Miraculous Draught of Fishes,' the 'Pasce oves meas,' 'St. Peter and St. John curing the Lame Man,' the 'Death of Ananias,' 'Elymas struck with Blindness,' 'Paul and Barnabas at Lystra,' and 'Paul preaching at Athens'—all large water-colour paintings, wonderfully grand in design, and for the most part still retaining a marvellous clearness and freshness of colouring. The cartoons representing the 'Stoning of

---

* See Appendix, note cxvii.
† Now in the Museum at South Kensington.

Stephen,' the 'Conversion of St. Paul,' and 'St. Paul in the Prison at Philippi,' have been lost. Raphael received for these cartoons 434 ducats in gold. He also prepared à cartoon for a tapestry, which has since been lost, and which was designed for the altar in the Sistine Chapel. The subject was the 'Coronation of the Virgin.' Twelve other cartoons for tapestries, representing events out of the life of Christ, and an allegorical representation of Religion, Justice, and Charity, of which but few fragments exist at the present day, were ordered by Francis I. of France, probably in 1519, on occasion of the canonisation of Francesco di Paolo, as an offering to the Church of St. Peter's. The subjects of these twelve cartoons were—the 'Murder of the Innocents' (forming three narrow tapestries), the 'Adoration of the Shepherds,' the 'Adoration of the Kings,' the 'Presentation in the Temple,' the 'Resurrection of Christ,' 'Christ appearing to Mary Magdalene,' 'Christ's Descent into Hell,' 'Christ speaking with the Disciples at Emmaus,' the 'Ascension of Christ,' and the 'Outpouring of the Holy Spirit.' As Raphael, however, died the year after the order, he had not advanced far in the work, and his pupil, Giulio Romano, undertook the completion of it in conjunction with others. The tapestries which were thus finished are also now hung up in the upper apartment of the Vatican, named after Pius V.

From the year 1515, Raphael was engaged in decorating the Stanza dell' Incendio with representations of the papal power; that is, partly with the miraculous power dwelling in the church itself, and partly with its sovereignty over all temporal authorities. Among these representations, the 'Incendio di Borgo'— that is, the burning of the quarter adjoining St. Peter's, called Borgo Nuovo, which took place during the pontificate of Leo IV.—is conspicuous above all for its dramatic interest, for its beauty of composition, and masterly power of execution. The three other wall-paintings in this stanza, which is also called the Sala di Torre Borgia, were for the most part executed by Raphael's pupils. They represent 'Leo the Tenth taking the oath,' the 'Coronation of Charlemagne,' and the 'Victory over the Saracens by Leo the Fourth, in the harbour of Ostia, not far from the mouth of the Tiber.' Besides these, there are six socle pictures and four small paintings in the window recesses, for the most part after designs by Giulio Romano.

In the Sala di Costantino, the wall paintings of which,

referring to the foundation of the temporal power of
the Popes under Constantine the Great, were not completed until after Raphael's death, the 'Victory of
Constantine over the opposition Emperor Maxentius on
the Ponte molle in Rome,' was executed by Giulio
Romano from a design of Raphael's. Raphael also
sketched a drawing for 'Constantine's Address to his
Warriors,' and he made the cartoons for two allegorical
figures of 'Justice' and 'Mercy,' the latter of which was
also executed in oils by Giulio Romano and Francesco
Penni. On the other hand, in the 'Baptism of Constantine,' in the 'Donation of Rome to Pope Sylvester,' and
in the eight Popes, with the other fourteen allegorical
figures and socle pictures, he took no part at all. Of
all these fresco paintings, the 'Battle of Constantine' is
by far the most important as regards its artistic merit.
It presents, as Vischer* strikingly remarks, a combination of all classes of imagination ; we see in it the mind
of the dramatic poet in the great crisis represented ; we
see historical fancy blended with pure human feeling
in the beautiful group of father and son; we see sublime fancy blended with beautiful simplicity in the

* See Appendix, note cxviii.

youth who belongs to this group; lastly, we see the creation of an animated action rich in figures, the grasping of a vast material with the clearest arrangement, so that, even in the wildest tumult of the fight, distinct groups are always to be seen, and there is nowhere a confusion, such as that in Rubens's ' Last Judgment' in Munich. Only Constantine himself is seated too far on his horse, a fault which often appears in others of Raphael's horsemen, and which probably proceeded from that want of power in animal-painting to which we have before referred.

Of the apostles and saints in the Sala de' Palafrenieri (an ante-room for the papal household, decorated by Giovanni da Udine with representations of the menagerie of Leo X.) nothing is now in existence, though Marc Anton's engravings have preserved the figures of the apostles. These apostles and saints were, according to Vasari's statement,* sketched by Raphael himself, and were executed in niches on a green ground.

For the sake of completeness, the droll designs must be mentioned which Raphael placed on the gate leading from the Stanza della Segnatura to the

* See Appendix, note cxix.

Stanza di Torre Borgia. The story upon which they are based is the following :—The Abbé Baraballo, a vain improvisatore, who considered himself a greater poet than Petrarch, was ordered by Pope Leo X., in ridicule, to ride upon an elephant, amid drums and trumpets, to the Capitol, to be crowned there as poet. At the bridge of St. Angelo, however, the animal threw the hero, and the latter must have been glad enough to get away with nothing worse than alarm and insult.

We know, moreover, from the Modenese records which we before mentioned,* that Raphael himself painted the decorations for a comedy, to be performed at the Vatican in the presence of the Pope. At La Magliana, a papal hunting-seat about five miles from Rome, close by the Tiber, a fresco painting, now partially destroyed, was executed at Leo X.'s command by one of Raphael's best pupils, after a design by the master. This painting represented the torture of St. Felicitas, and it·has been engraved by Marc Anton. The work belongs probably to the last few years of Raphael's life.

* See Appendix, note cxx.

Ever since the middle of the fifteenth century, the higher efforts of study in Italy had been directed almost entirely to classic antiquity, and hence, in noble natures, a considerable extension of view and a life full of mind and feeling had been produced; whilst lesser souls drew from it the germ of moral destruction, inasmuch as they regarded the new atmosphere, as is always the case, as a convenient cloak under which they could free themselves from the Christian principles of a strict morality, and give the reins to their unbridled lusts. We must take this circumstance into consideration, if we would understand the character of the court of Leo X., and the manifold influences which the artist Raphael received from the different prominent members of the papal society. Immediately after the commencement of Leo X.'s Pontificate, he once more met his friend from Urbino, the Count Baldassare Castiglione of Casatico near Mantua, the gifted author of the famous work 'Il Cortegiano,'* in which the ideal of refined society is depicted, and a man who soon became the centre of a distinguished circle, on account of his active zeal for art and science.

* See Appendix, note cxxi.

The Pope treated him with the greatest distinction, as a polished courtier and an ambassador from the Duke of Urbino, and Raphael painted his portrait, it appears, twice—once the head alone, uncovered, and once a half-length one. The former is now in the Palace Torlonia, in Rome; the other, by far the superior, is in the Louvre. Another very intimate friend of Raphael's was the learned Pietro Bembo, whom Leo X. appointed as his secretary in the year 1513, and who was subsequently made a cardinal by Pope Paul III. His Latin prose and poetry were considered to bear a resemblance to that of Cicero and Virgil, and his Italian style reminded his readers of Boccaccio and Petrarca.* He remained in Rome till the year 1519, and through him Raphael became acquainted with the two distinguished Venetian authors, Andrea Navagero and Agostino Beazzano, whose portraits he painted for him in the spring of 1516. The original picture, painted on wood, seems to have utterly disappeared, but a second likeness on canvas, which Passavant is inclined to regard as the work of a Venetian, is in the Palace Doria in Rome.† Raphael was also on terms

---

* See Appendix, note cxxii. † See Appendix, note cxxiii.

of intimacy with the three greatest poets of his time, Lodovico Ariosto, Jacopo Sannazzaro, and Antonio Tebaldeo. With the first, who was probably only once in Rome after the accession of Leo X., he carried on a correspondence; while the two latter, who were summoned to Rome by Leo, lived there in constant intercourse with him. In the year 1516, he painted Tebaldeo in oils; the portrait, however, is lost. Sannazzaro also was painted by him; yet the half-length and much retouched portrait of a man of about sixty years of age, with a black cap on his long white hair and in a simple black coat with a narrow white collar, which in 1850 came into the possession of the Emperor of Russia on the sale of the art-treasures of King William II. at the Hague, is not the long and vainly sought for original; a fact which Dr. Waagen has convincingly proved in his treatise published in 1864 at Munich, entitled 'The Paintings in the Imperial Hermitage at St. Petersburg.' Both poets were placed by Raphael in his fresco painting of the 'Parnassus.' *

Among the noble patrons of our artist, we must mention the Cardinals Giulio de' Medici, Bernardo

---

* See Appendix, note cxxiv.

Divizio da Bibbiena, Raphael Riario, Baldassare Turini da Pescia, and Giovanni Battista Branconio of Aquila. He even appointed the two latter as executors of his will. Giulio de' Medici, a natural son of Giuliano, the brother of Leo X., ascended the papal chair in 1523 as Clement VIII. Raphael has immortalised him *al fresco* in his wall painting, the 'Victory over the Saracens,' and also in that famous knee-piece of Pope Leo X., which he painted in oils about the year 1518, where he is placed with the Cardinal de' Rossi. This picture, which is now in the Pitti Palace, is one of his most distinguished portraits, unsurpassed especially in the natural imitation of the details of the dress. Many other of Raphael's best works, which we have yet to mention, we owe to the orders of this grave and good man.

It is probable that he painted the wise statesman-like Bibbiena twice in oils: one portrait of him is now in the Museum at Madrid; the other, executed for the most part by the hand of a pupil, is in the Pitti Palace. As Bibbiena lived in the upper story of the Vatican, over Raphael's Loggie, and possessed no house of his own, he commissioned Raphael, in 1516, to decorate his bath-room (called, for no intelligible

K

reason, 'il retiro di Giuseppe,' although this portion
of the palace was not built until after Julius's death)
with mythological representations, painted, after the
taste of the ancients, on a dark reddish-brown ground.
Raphael, however, only furnished the sketches, and
certainly not even all of these. The 'Birth of Venus,'
'Venus and Cupid riding on Dolphins,' 'Venus com-
plaining to Cupid of her Wounds,' 'Venus drawing a
Thorn from her Foot,' 'Six Cupids as Conquerors,' and
'Cupid and Pan,' betray certainly a true Raphael-like
grace; whilst 'Venus and Adonis,' as well as 'Jupiter
and Antiope,' lead us to infer the hand of Giulio
Romano; and 'Vulcan and Pallas' even of some less
talented pupil. Much of it is destroyed; the ceiling
pictures are scarcely now to be recognised. What
approval these representations met with is not only
testified by the engravings of Marc Anton, which were
executed at the time, but also by the beautiful repe-
tition of them in the old vestibule of the Villa Pala-
tina, at that time probably belonging to the Duca
Mattei, and now to the Englishman, Mr. Mills. They
are all executed *al fresco* by Giulio Romano.

Lastly, in the court of Leo X., there was the
librarian Tommaso Inghirami, a man distinguished

for his learning, and belonging to a noble family of
Volterra. He had been appointed Bishop of Ragusa
in 1510 by Julius II.; he had performed the duties
of secretary in the conclave in which Leo X. was
elected Pope; and he bore the surname of Phædra,
because in the performance of Seneca's tragedy of
' Hippolytus,' in which he had played the part of
Phædra, he had distinguished himself by his extraordinary presence of mind. When something acci-
dentally fell into disorder in the machinery, and the
performance of the play was in consequence interrupted, he entertained the spectators so well by his
improvised Latin verses that they clapped the loudest
applause. Raphael painted an excellent portrait of
this somewhat portly man in 1513, in the red dress
of the office he held in the conclave. The light is
managed almost in Holbein's manner. The painting
is now an ornament of the Pitti Palace.

The portrait of a violin-player, bearing the date of
the year 1518, now in the Palace Sciarra Colonna in
Rome, is most attractive from its grace and beauty.
It probably represents Andrea Marone of Brescia, also
a favourite companion of the Pope, who delighted in
his improvisations on the bass-viol. At about the

same time, or rather earlier, the following portraits were executed by Raphael: that of a Cardinal (Borgia?), in the Borghese Palace in Rome; that of the Archdeacon Frederic Carondelet, in the Duke of Grafton's possession, in London; that of a young man, in the possession of the Duke of Alba, in Madrid; and some others, regarding which some uncertainty prevails as to Raphael's share in their execution.

We may as well at once mention here the other portraits of the Medicean family which Raphael painted. There is the half-length figure of Lorenzo de' Medici, Duke of Urbino, executed in 1518, but only now existing in copies at Florence and Montpellier; and the half-length portrait, executed probably in 1514, of his brother Giuliano, the youngest brother of Leo X., who had the command of the papal troops in Rome, and who died in 1516. The original of this also is lost; a copy of it, by Allori, is now in the Uffizi, in Florence. Lastly, Raphael also painted the little Hippolito de' Medici, the natural son of Giuliano, as a page, in the fresco picture of the 'Coronation of Charlemagne.'

Vischer has beautifully expressed in what the principal charm of the portraits of Raphael lies. 'Raphael,' he says,* 'has a magic charm in his lines, an undulating grace, an oval form in his heads, an inclination, a leaning of the head and neck, an outline of figure, hands, and legs, and in all this an expression of heavenly love and purity of being, which belongs to himself alone, and can never return again. With this guide of the law of beauty in his hand, he is absolutely sure to adhere to the line of truth, even when depicting individual traits; and while hitherto this point had been more carefully cultivated by the Florentine school than by that of Umbria, which surpassed it in many other respects, it was now this very man, an Umbrian, who stood highest even in this also, and by further extension and development of that which Leonardo da Vinci had done before him, formed in the Italian style that absolute standard for the union of normal beauty with individual traits. The essentially characteristic portrait-like traits in different men could not have been transformed into beauty with more wonderful expulsion of all that is unessential, accidental, and disturbing to the grandeur of the style. The true portrait assisted him in this,

* See Appendix, note cxxv.

that while he refined it, he yet brought it into closer empirical similarity. His colour he took, in all its warmth of feeling, from his master (Perugino), bringing it in his portraits to the perfection of Venetian colouring; this, however, only in a few, for on this point a new way was opened for his adoption.'

In resuming the chronological series of Raphael's works, after this digression, we must first mention the four 'Prophets' and 'Sibyls,' in fresco, ordered by Agostino Chigi, a rich merchant of Siena, for a chapel in the church of Santa Maria della Pace in Rome, and which probably were begun in 1514. If he did not attain in these to the grand and original manner of Michael Angelo, he yet decidedly surpassed his rival in the beauty of his forms, especially as regards the 'Sibyls.' The 'Sibyls' were placed over an arch to the right, at the entrance to the church: there were, enumerating them from left to right, the Cumæan Sibyl, the Persian, the Phrygian, and the old Tiburtine—all represented, in harmony with the nature of the master, as lovely Greek Muses; while Michael Angelo had conceived them as beings of remote antiquity, as mighty and gigantic prophetesses of ancient and mysterious wisdom.* The 'Prophets,' in the upper division of the chapel, on the wall of the arch leading to the altar, above the 'Sibyls,' represented Daniel with roll, David in his sacerdotal habits, Jonah looking up s heaven, and Hosea sitting down. They were all executed by Timoteo Viti after Raphael's cartoons.

Göthe has with justice rectified Volkmann's verdict, when he said of the 'Sibyls:' 'The drawing is accurate, but the composition weak, though probably this may be attributed to the inconvenience of their position.' To this Göthe replied, in his 'Italienische Reise:'† 'Raphael was never fettered by the space allowed him by the architecture; it far rather belongs to the greatness and grace of his genius, that he understood how to fill and to decorate every space in the most ornamental manner, as he conspicuously proved in the Farnesina. Even the splendid pictures of the 'Mass of Bolsèna,' the 'Deliverance of the imprisoned St. Peter,' and the 'Parnassus' would not have been as invaluable as they are, without the wonderful restriction of the space that contains them. Equally

* See Appendix, note cxxvi.   † See Appendix, note cxxvii.

so with the "Sibyls," the concealed symmetry on which
everything in the composition depends is executed
in the most gifted manner; for as in the organism
of nature, so in art also, the perfection of life is
exhibited within the narrowest limits.'

To the same year belongs the fresco of the 'Galatea,'
which Raphael painted in the hall of the house built
by Baldassare Peruzzi for Agostino Chigi, now the Villa
Farnesina of the ex-King of Naples. Vasari * has
placed the representations from the fable of Cupid and
Psyche, in the Loggia of the same villa, among the
works at the end of our artist's career; but probably,
with the exception of one very beautiful Grace seen
from the back, in the picture where Cupid is showing
his beloved one to the Graces, they were all executed
in fresco by Giulio Romano, Francesco Penni, and
Giovanni da Udine, after the cartoons of the master.
The 'Galatea,' on the other hand, is almost entirely the
work of his own hand, and it is equally charming from
the beauty of the design, and the exact and admirable
symmetry of the arrangement, as from the brightness
and cheerfulness of the colouring, and the lively natu-

* See Appendix, note cxxviii.

ralness of the representation. The figure of 'Galatea' surpasses perhaps everything which we possess in beautiful and nude female forms; it is therefore especially interesting to learn from a letter which Raphael wrote to his patron, the Count of Castiglione, that, for want of a beautiful model, he created this figure from a certain idea of beauty which hovered before his mind. ' With regard to the Galatea,' thus he writes in this letter (which is otherwise worthy of notice, and we shall refer to it again), ' I should consider myself a great artist if half the beautiful things were true which your lordship writes to me, but I recognise in your praises the love you bear me. I must say, *that to paint a beautiful woman, I ought to see many such,* and, moreover, I ought to have your lordship near me to assist me with your judgment. *As, however, both good judges and beautiful women are rare, I have worked upon a certain idea that presents itself to my mind.* Whether this idea possesses any artistic excellence, I know not; but I have done my best to attain it.'

We can well imagine the extent of useless æsthetical talk which this apparent acknowledgment of Raphael's absolute idealism has caused. In my own opinion the great painter, full of all that Italian gentilezza which

expressed itself in refined and polite flattery towards
his noble patron, only intended to say what everyone
feels who examines deeply into his works, namely, that
with his art it was no slavish imitation of the forms of
nature, but a power of representing an idea conceived
by him, according to the forms which the visible
creation exhibits 'as consistent with its spiritual
nature;' in a word, it was 'the pourtrayal of a world
idealised in beauty.' *   Art imitates nature, as we all
know, but at the same time she goes far beyond her, in
that she realises that which nature cannot always
succeed in realising.   Thus wrote also Federigo Zuccharo: 'Soleva dire Raffaelo che il pittore ha obbligo
di far le cose non come le fa la natura, mà come ella le
dovrebbe fare.' †

Soon after, in the year 1515, Raphael painted 'St.
Cecilia' for the chapel founded by the subsequently
canonised Elena Duglioli del Oglio, in the church
of San Giovanni in Monte: the painting is now
in the Pinacoteca at Bologna.   This picture, which is
seven feet three inches high and four feet six inches
broad, is among the most admired creations of the
master.   Göthe thus significantly expressed himself

* See Appendix, note cxxix.   † See Appendix, note cxxx.

respecting it, October 18, 1786 : * '*He* (that is, Raphael) *always exactly achieves what others would wish
to achieve,* and I will not now say more regarding
this painting than that it is by him. There are five
saints there side by side, who in nowise concern us,
but whose existence is so perfect that we wish the
picture could endure for ever, until we also are ready
for departure.' This splendid picture is, however, unfortunately even now in a deplorable condition, having
been much injured and shamefully retouched in Paris
in the year 1803, when it was transferred from panel to
canvas; a fact which Passavant scarcely sufficiently
brings forward and acknowledges in his work, when
speaking of this painting (i. 254-256; ii. 180-183;
iii. 123-124), although his attention was specially
drawn to it by the artistic engraver, Professor Eugen
Eduard Schäffer, at Frankfort on the Main, who has
minutely studied the Bolognese original, and has nar-
rowly discussed its Parisian history. Most truly can
we assent to Nagler's verdict upon this painting: † 'It
is full of calm devotion, like the solemn long-drawn
tones of old church melodies;' still we must not forget,
when we see the present condition of this work of art,

---

* See Appendix, note cxxxi.   † See Appendix, note cxxxii.

what Rumohr wrote respecting it even in 1831,* therefore long before Passavant, in words that are full of truth :
' This work is indeed at the present day so injured by
its restorer, that it is more like a copy than an original.'
Only in the head of St. Augustine do we still see the
true power and uniqueness of Raphael's brush. Among
the many copies that exist, the one now in the possession of Mr. Thomas du Boulay at Sandgate, in Kent,†
occupies a conspicuous place. It is very carefully
painted, and the detail is minutely executed. Professor
Schäffer ascribes it to Agostino Caracci for weighty
reasons :‡ it is executed, he says, on a smaller size,
and does not entirely reach the expression that lies
in the heads of the original, and often, as for example
in the figure of St. Paul, even wilfully differs from the
painting. This latter diversity seems to have been
caused by the desire to increase the impression produced by the original. Not unimportant is the fact
that Raphael followed pretty accurately in the execution of the picture the original sketch engraved by
Marc Anton, the complete genuineness of which, more-

---

* See Appendix, note cxxxiii.   † See Appendix, note cxxxiv.
‡ See Appendix, note cxxxv.

over, Passavant considers doubtful;* but nevertheless he happily departed from his original idea in the three male figures, St. Paul, St. John, and St. Augustine. In the sketch they appeared to him too separate, and without the necessary relation to the principal figure; in the painting, therefore, he connected them more closely with the true point of his conception. With respect to the 'Magdalene,' also, he departed from his sketch, which represents the saint in profile, looking up with transport to the angelic glory, whilst in the painting she appears turned *en face* to the spectator; truly, as Nagler remarks,† 'without showing any interest in the deeper emotion which fills the minds of all around her,' as they see St. Cecilia completely elevated in listening to the harmonies of heaven.

At this same time the artist sent the 'Vision of Ezekiel,' now in the Pitti Palace, to Bologna, to the Count Vincenzo Ercolani. In spite of its small size, this picture produces a grand effect; the influence of Michael Angelo in the composition is unmistakable. A 'Birth of Christ,' which Raphael painted for Count Canossa in Verona, is now lost. Paul Veronese and

* See Appendix, note cxxxvi. † See Appendix, note cxxxvii.

Taddeo Zuccharo are said to have made copies from it, which, however, are likewise nowhere to be found. To the same period, too, belong the frescoes with which Raphael, in conjunction with others, adorned his villa in the park of the Villa Borghese. This villa was entirely destroyed in the revolution in the year 1848; happily, however, the Prince Borghese had removed, in 1844, the three best frescoes of the third smaller apartment, and had had them framed in his gallery at Rome. One of them alone, the 'Marriage of Alexander with Roxana,' is Raphael's own composition; the two other pictures are ascribed to Michael Angelo and Perino del Vaga. Göthe, who saw the villa while it was still un-destroyed, remarks that 'the little genii and full-grown men painted on the walls, playing antics on scrolls and mouldings, moving merrily to balance themselves, apparently hurrying after some end, and doing all that a love of motion can inspire,' seemed to him more in the spirit of the antique than all Raphael's other arabesques; and he adds: 'It is all the more charming, because he might have done so much here, but he chose to do but little, and just what was sufficient.' *

* See Appendix, note cxxxviii.

We must here again interrupt our enumeration of the Raphael paintings, that we may give some brief mention of his architectural and plastic works, for, like Michael Angelo, Leonardo da Vinci, and the German Albrecht Dürer, with whom he also stood on terms of the most friendly and respectful intercourse, and exchanged presents, his genius embraced all three branches of the plastic art. Respecting the architectural works of our master, a special volume appeared under the title, 'Opere architettoniche di Raffaelo Sanzio incise e dichiarate dell' architetto Carlo Pontani' (Rome, 1845). It consists of thirty-six sheets, the two last of which, however, as Passavant has shown,* decidedly do not contain architectural plans designed by Raphael.

When Raphael had gained great consideration and wealth in Rome, and had gathered round him a number of superior pupils, and had begun to receive commissions from all parts of Italy, he designed, with the assistance of Bramante, his countryman and relative, at that time architect of St. Peter's Church, a plan for a two-storied house for himself, which he

* See Appendix, note cxxxix.

built entirely of brick, in 1513, in the Borgo Nuovo, opposite the church of St. Peter's. According to Vasari's description in the ' Life of Bramante,' * this was ' a very beautiful and new invention,' thus to use brick and mortar ('lavorato di mattoni e di getto con casse '), instead of hewn stone in architectural structures. In the year 1514, Raphael took possession of his house. The principal façade faced the square of St. Peter's. The lower story, built in rustic style, had five arches, the central one of which contained the entrance door, while the two others on each side led to the stores. The second story, with five windows, with pediments and balustrades, was adorned with rows of coupled pillars of the Doric order, half-projecting, and standing on pedestals, and a capital of the same order crowned the whole. This façade, according to the proportions added to the engraving published in 1549 by Antonio Lafreri,† was a hundred and four palms broad, the ground floor was twenty-nine palms high, and the upper story thirty-four palms and six inches high. Only the lower part of the right corner pillar is now to be seen of the

* See Appendix, note cxl. † See Appendix, note cxli.

building, which is almost entirely destroyed. The remainder has been partly rebuilt, partly incorporated with the Palazzo Accoromboni. Raphael bequeathed the house to his patron, Cardinal Bibbiena, who was in no wise wealthy; he, however, died soon after Raphael (November 9, 1520), and therefore never inhabited it.*

After the death of Bramante, Pope Leo X., in accordance with the desire of the dying man, appointed Raphael by a brief dated August 1, 1514, architect of St. Peter's, with a salary of three hundred ducati d' oro; this, however, did not occur until after the artist had sent in a model, which excited general admiration, and an estimate of the cost of the building; thus proving his especial ability for such an office. Raphael's model has unhappily been lost, and the ground plan alone is given us by Sebastiano Serlio in the third book of his work, published by Scamozzi, 'Tutte l' Opere d' Architettura' (Venice, 1545, second edition, 1584). It is also to be found in plate 10 of Philippo Bonanni's 'Numismata summorum Pontificum Templi Vaticani Fabricam indicantia' (Rome,

* See Appendix, note cxlii.

1696), but it is here erroneously assigned to Bramante. Passavant * thinks that the plan, which is to
be found in the pamphlet in the Barberini Palace, containing architectural drawings by Giuliano da San Gallo,
has in it Raphael's first design. According to this, the
ground plan forms a Latin cross, with seven naves the
length of the building, the central one of which is
broad, and the three narrow naves on each side have
an outlet into the vestibule. The choir is surrounded
by a wall built in a half-circle, leaving a private
passage between the outer surrounding walls, while
the tribunes of the side aisles, furnished with niches,
each, describe a small half-circle, formed by two
pilasters and twelve pillars in groups of four together.
The vestibule rests on thirty pillars (Serlio says thirty-
six); only those at the extreme ends are coupled.
The pillars along the church are strengthened by
double pilasters, with niches between them.

On the whole, this design is less free and grand
than that given by Serlio, but even had this been
followed, St. Peter's Church would have been more
beautiful, and more in accordance with the taste of the

* See Appendix, note cxliii,

ancients, than in its present architecture, which is un‐
compact and heavy in parts, and a pure style is in no
degree preserved in its detail. The effect of Raphael's
plan would undoubtedly have been richer, and yet at
the same time calmer; and standing before the church,
the dome would have been at least seen, as the vesti‐
bule would have been lower, although even according
to this plan it would have been placed rather far
behind. Now, as is well known, the dome, in spite of
its immense dimensions, is concealed from the eye of
the spectator standing before the front façade. We
must, nevertheless, allow that Raphael was in error
when he introduced the ground plan of a Latin cross
instead of that of the Greek, proposed by Bramante,
and subsequently with the utmost energy by Michael
Angelo also; for the latter was in harmony with the
whole idea of the building, and although Raphael's
plan was never executed, that frequent wavering
between the two ground plans, which may be ascribed
to his influence, has materially injured the effect of
the building in its final completion.* How much
Raphael's plan differed in all parts from that of

* See Appendix, note cxliv.

Bramante is shown by a medal, which Cardosso executed in 1506.*

　The delight of our master at his new office is manifested in the letter addressed to his uncle Ciarla on July 1, 1514, therefore previous to the completion of his appointment as architect of the cathedral—the same letter in which he expresses himself so freely with regard to his disinclination to marriage. 'With respect to my residence in Rome,' he writes,† 'my love for the building of St. Peter's Church would always prevent my remaining anywhere but here, for I have now Bramante's place. What city in the world, however, is more worthy than Rome? What undertaking more noble than that of St. Peter's? For this is the first temple in the world and the greatest building ever seen, and it will cost more than a million of money. Imagine, the Pope has set aside 60,000 ducats yearly for the building, and he thinks of nothing else. He has given me an associate in a monk of great experience, a man more than eighty years old, and as the Pope sees that he can live but a short time, and he has the reputation of great learn-

---

* See Appendix, note cxlv.　　　　　† See Appendix, note cxlvi.

ing, His Holiness has resolved to associate him with me as an assistant, so that I may learn from him any secret in architecture which he may possess, and thus become more and more perfect in the art.* His name is Fra Giocondo. The Pope summons us to his presence every day, and speaks with us respecting the building.'

Far more beautifully does Raphael express himself respecting the building of St. Peter's in the letter to Count Castiglione, which we have before quoted, and in which he speaks of the ideal of the beautiful. 'Our holy father,' he there says, 'has laid a great burden on my shoulders in the honour he has shown me, in giving me the superintendence of the building of St. Peter's. I hope, indeed, I shall not sink under it. My chief confidence is that the model, which I made of it, has pleased His Holiness, and has been approved by many men of cultivated minds. But I carry my aspirations still higher: *I would fain revive the beautiful forms of the buildings of antiquity,* but I know not whether the fate of Icarus is before me. Vitruvius affords me some light, but not enough.' †

* See Appendix, note cxlvii.   † See Appendix, note cxlviii.

From this we plainly see, and it is elsewhere confirmed, that Raphael, equally with Michael Angelo,
ranked the art of the ancients far beyond his own,
but that he lacked the true means for arriving at
a full understanding of Greek architecture, since at
the time in which he lived they were possessed by
none. 'Vitruvius' was translated into Italian by the
learned Marco Fabio Calvo, to aid him in his conscientious studies. The manuscript, containing mar-
ginal notes in his own handwriting, is now in the
possession of the Library at Munich.

A further proof of how great an interest Raphael
took in the office entrusted to him, of architect of the
cathedral, is the well-known papal brief of August 27,
1515,* in which, at his suggestion, the means were
given into his hands for procuring, at a reasonable
price, the stone necessary for the building of St.
Peter's, all Romans being prohibited, upon pain of
100 to 300 gold scudi, from hewing or appropriating
any stone dug from the ruins of Rome, without previously informing Raphael, and receiving his permission. In the same manner, the Roman stonemasons
especially were not to manufacture antique blocks of

* See Appendix, note cxlix.

marble with carved inscriptions unless Raphael had previously given his approval. By this means he managed to exercise a control over all the excavations in Rome, and thus to save many monuments of ancient art, which now constitute the ornaments of the museums of the city. It was even before he entered upon his office, an office which we may justly desig_ nate as that of a preserver of Roman antiquities, that the 'Laocoon' group (1506), the 'Apollo Belvidere,' the 'Torso of the Hercules,' and the groups of the 'Nile' and the 'Tiber,' as well as many others, were discovered and placed in the Vatican.

Thus ever deeper and deeper did Raphael advance in the study of the Roman antiquities, and in the few last years of his life he was even engaged in a project, perhaps in common with his patron Castiglione, for making a complete plan of old Rome, and for restoring the ancient buildings according to the remains still in existence, and the descriptions left of them by old authors in ground plans and sketches. The interest which this projec, met with in·Rome is shown, among many others, by the epigram of Cölio Calcagnini of Ferrara : *

* See Appendix, note cl.

weak a foundation, owing to the hurry to which Bramante had been urged by Julius II.'s impetuosity. Raphael, therefore, lost much time at first in increasing the strength of these pillars, and afterwards the money for the building of the church became more and more sparingly given, consumed as it was by Leo X.'s extravagant love of splendour, and his war against the Duke of Urbino.* More fortunate was our artist in the completion of another building, also begun by Bramante, namely, the court in the Vatican called San Damaso. For this, too, he drew a richer and more beautiful plan, and had a model of it executed in wood. Even at the present day this court is universally admired. It is open on the one side, and has a three-sided simple arcade on the ground floor, built of brick ; the three upper stories being in travertino marble, with half-projecting pillars, first of the Doric and then of the Ionic order, a row of detached Corinthian pillars crowning the whole. Here are the Loggie, each of which has a small dome, corresponding with the arch.

Among the other plans designed by Raphael is that

---

* See Appendix, note clii.

for the chapel in Santa Maria del Popolo at Rome, which he executed for his friend Agostino Chigi, and which was not entirely completed until after the artist's death; also that for the façade of the church of San Lorenzo in Florence, which was never executed, and for which Michael Angelo also prepared a competition design. (Raphael must, therefore, have travelled to Florence in the winter of 1515–16, expressly at the Pope's command.) There is also the plan for the Palace Coltrolini, near St. Andrea della Valle, now the Palazzo Vidoni; the plan for the Casa di Jacopo Sadoleto, now Casa Berti, at the end of the Borgo Nuovo, on the right of the square of St. Peter's; it is built in brick, and has a façade of five windows. He also designed the plan for the villa of the Cardinal Giulio de' Medici, on the Monte Mario, now Villa Madama; as well as those for the Palace Pandolfini, in the street of San Gallo in Florence, and for the Casa Uguccioni in the same place, both of which were executed during his residence in Florence, in the winter of 1515–16. The first-mentioned palace was, however, not built until after Raphael's death, when it was consigned to Bastiano Aristotile da San Gallo.* Lastly,

* See Appendix, note cliii.

there was the palace of Giovanni Battista Branconio d' Aquila, erected opposite St. Peter's, but afterwards pulled down on the enlargement of the latter building. It was decorated with stucco-work by Giovanni da Udine, and Vasari speaks of it as ' cosa bellissima.' Of the other plans which have been also ascribed to Raphael— namely, that for the church San Giovanni Battista dei Fiorentini in Rome; that for the restoration of the church of Santa Maria e Dominica, also called Della Navicella, on the Monte Celio ; and, lastly, that for the stables of Agostino Chigi, near the Farnesina—we know as good as nothing.*

In order briefly to characterise the direction which Raphael pursued as an architect, we will take Passavant's opinion, and say that he possessed, far more than his teacher and countryman Bramante, a just feeling for great architectural masses and divisions, and a taste for beautiful relations and forms, which was quite peculiar to himself. To his architectural structures, to his cornices, windows, and doors, he gave more richness than Bramante did. He was fond of lintels over windows, to increase the picturesque effect, and to give

* See Appendix, note cliv.

his architecture a richer stamp, alternately covering them with pointed and rounded pediments, placing double pillars, and breaking the socle by projecting window-ledges. Nevertheless, his cornices and plinths always run in an unbroken line, so that they are in no wise prejudicial to the effect of harmonious repose. His style of architecture is decidedly purer than that of Michael Angelo. Baldassare Peruzzi alone, of all the architects of the sixteenth century, could dispute precedence with him.*

Undoubtedly we owe to Raphael's abundance of rich and noble ornament the revival of the insipid renaissance style, whilst from Michael Angelo's powerful character an indisputably wilder style proceeded: those gigantic pilasters and entablatures, those angular forms, the breaking and intersecting of pediments over doors and windows, the introduction of scrolls in curved and twisted ornaments — changes which at length gradually gave place to the rococo style, to the school of Bernini and Borromini, ' the deadly enemy,' as it were, ' of the straight line.'†

But as regards architecture also, the universality of

* See Appendix, note clv.   † See Appendix, note clvi.

Raphael's genius appears not to have been exhausted to
the utmost in the productions which history assigns to
him; for it is more than probable that he attempted
sculpture also. We have every reason to suppose that
the magnificent marble statue of the prophet Jonah,
in the chapel of Agostino Chigi, in Santa Maria del
Popolo, was executed by him, while for the statue of
Elias, which Lorenzetto made, he certainly furnished
the design. Moreover, it appears from a letter of
Count Castiglione's to his attorney, Andrea Piperario,
in Rome, dated May 8, 1523,* that the life-size marble
group of the boy fatally wounded, lying on the back of a
dolphin, who is holding him fast by his long-falling hair,
was executed at all events after Raphael's own design,
though with Lorenzetto's assistance.† There are,
too, many designs of Raphael's for bowls, medals, and
similar things; and Passavant considers it, moreover,
as certain, that the beautiful Fontana delle Tartarughe
(with the tortoise), in Rome, was executed after a
model of Raphael's. ‡

Lastly, Professor Andreas Müller,§ the keeper of the

---

* See Appendix, note clvii.
† It is now at Down Hill, in Ireland.
‡ See Appendix, note clviii., note clix., and note clx.
§ See Appendix, note clxi.

collection of the Art Academy at Düsseldorf, has attempted, in a small pamphlet, which appeared in 1860, to prove with reasons which have hitherto remained unrefuted, so far as I know, that Raphael also understood the use of the graver and the file, and, therefore, not merely, according to the traditional supposition, greatly assisted Marc Anton in many engravings which the latter executed from his compositions and under his direction, sometimes even correcting the outline; but that he also must be reckoned among the *peintres graveurs*, that is, those who have engraved for themselves, such as Dürer, Francia, and many others of his contemporaries. There is, for instance, in the collection of the Düsseldorf Academy, an engraving six inches four lines high, and two inches eight lines broad, according to Paris measure, representing the Holy Virgin sitting on clouds, holding with her right hand the Infant Saviour, who is leaning against her, and surrounded by four boy angels, who are looking out from the clouds. The composition, perhaps a first sketch for the 'Madonna di Fuligno,' which it strongly resembles, is certainly full of a peculiar Raphael-like grace, and the execution so plainly surpasses that of the well-known engraving of Marc Anton, which Bartsch ('Peintre

Graveur,' xiv. 47) and Passavant (a. a. O. ii. 636, No. 19) mention, as well as all the other engravings, which this artist has made from Raphael's original drawings, that Müller has arrived at the conviction that Raphael himself engraved this *one* sheet, and this (which he considers very probable) because he was incited to do so by the engravings which Albert Dürer sent to him in Rome about the year 1510, and among which was probably the beautiful ' Holy Family with the Butterfly.' Raphael's engraving resembles this in the most remarkable manner, in tone and composition, and even in the management of the different parts, as, for example, in the clouds, the heads and hands, in the representation of the deep red by simple strokes, and so forth, so that we have reason to believe that Raphael wished to test his own capability by this engraving of Dürer's, in producing a similarly picturesque effect by the application of similar means.

Vasari relates in a passage in the Florentine edition of 1550* (a passage subsequently omitted, but again inserted in the new Trieste edition), that Raphael had seen Dürer's engraving as the latter was going to his work,

---

* See Appendix, note clxii.

was at once animated by the desire to show what he also could produce in this art; he had therefore prepared many studies in it for Marc Antonio Raimondi of Bologna, at that time the most famous engraver in Italy; and as these had succeeded, he had his early things, such as the 'Murder of the Innocents,' the 'Last Supper,' and others, printed by him. From this certainly not very concise passage, Müller also infers that Raphael at first attempted to engrave his own works, because the proofs which Marc Antonio brought with him from Bologna to Rome did not satisfy him; hence before he entrusted the latter with his manifold works, he made him prepare some engravings after those of Albert Dürer under his own direction, so that he might perfect himself in the technical part of the art of engraving. No sketch of Raphael's, after which Marc Antonio might have engraved his plate, is extant. Müller is far more of opinion that the Marc Antonio engraving, which has been often copied, must have been prepared direct from a copy of the same plate, a proof sheet of which the Düsseldorf Academy possesses from the bequest of Carlo Maratti (through its subsequent director, Lambert Krahe, who gained a great part of the Maratti

M

collection of sketches). That Raphael had, even before this, given great attention to the art of engraving is proved by the account of Lodovico Dolce,* according to which the artist, even before Dürer's engravings had reached him, had hung up many engravings by German masters in his atelier, and was wont to extol them highly. He had, moreover, the engravings' of Mantegna, which he highly esteemed, and which he had long known, and had even himself copied them.† That he did not, however, continue to practise the art of engraving is easily explained, for it was exactly from the year 1510 that he was commissioned to execute such an overwhelming amount of artistic work of another kind. We have only desired to show that in this art also he possessed the capability for excelling.

We will now return to the painter Raphael, and omitting the portraits, which we have before enumerated all together, we will briefly glance at the great master-works which he created during the few last years of his life.

The date of the 'Madonna della Sedia,' the ornament of the Pitti Palace, is not accurately determined, but

---

* See Appendix, note clxiii.　　　† Ibid. note clxiv.

Rumohr places the completion of this painting, which is especially admired for the beauty of its colouring— certainly much too early—in the year 1510.* Similar in style is the 'Madonna della Tenda,' which derives its name from the arrangement of the background—a curtain with some sky on the right. Of the many re- presentations of this subject that are in existence, that in the Pinakothek at Munich, which was carried away by the French from Madrid, and was purchased from Sir Thomas Baring in 1814, by the then Crown Prince Louis of Bavaria, is considered as the original of Raphael. Nevertheless, even this copy could not have been entirely painted by Raphael's own hand, although the conception of the whole decidedly belongs to him.

The 'Bearing the Cross,' a painting nine feet ten inches high, and seven feet two inches broad, also called '*Lo Spasimo di Sicilia*,' because the picture was formerly in the monastery church of Santa Maria dello Spasimo, though it now forms the ornament of the Museum at Madrid, must certainly be reckoned among the best works of our master; and, owing to the masterly engravings of Paolo Toschi, it is among the

* See Appendix, note clxv.

M 2

most known of his productions. When we consider all it has gone through—the vessel, in which it was sent to Palermo, suffered shipwreck on the coast of Liguria, and the chest containing the picture was carried by the waves to Genoa—we can only be astonished at its general good preservation; but by the transmission from wood to 'canvass, which Bonnemaison effected, and the re-touching that followed this process, the colours have been injured not a little, as is the case with all the pictures exposed to this proceeding.

There is also in Madrid the ' Visitation,' a painting seven feet two inches high, and five feet five inches and ten lines broad, which Raphael, assisted perhaps by Giulio Romano, painted for the chapel of the Papal chamberlain, Giovanni Battista Branconio, in the church of San Silvestro, at Aquila, in the Abruzzi. In this painting, the head of the aged Elizabeth, the charming expression of modesty and humility in the figure of Mary, and the exquisitely-executed garments of both women, are full of effect; only the throat of Mary appears rather thin. The landscape in the background, with the anachronistic representation of the Baptism of Christ in the river Jordan, has much breadth in it.

Lastly, in the Madrid Museum, there are two other treasures of Raphael's—the 'Holy Family under the Oak-tree,' which in the Madrid catalogue is called 'La Sacra Familia del Agnus Dei,' while a very good copy of it in the Pitti Palace is called, on account of the lizard which appears in it, 'La Sacra Famiglia della Lacerta;' and the so-called 'Perla,' a very charming composition, which Raphael designed for the Duke Federigo di Mantova, though the execution of it in oils belongs for the most part to a pupil, probably to Giulio Romano, just as the composition of the above-named 'Holy Family' is ascribed to Francesco Penni. There are very evident traces that Raphael himself made many alterations in the 'Perla' before sending it away. Philip IV. of Spain bought the picture for two thousand pounds sterling, from the remains of the English King Charles I., who was beheaded.

For Francis I. of France, Raphael painted the 'Archangel Michael thrusting Satan down into the Abyss,' and the large 'Holy Family'—the Virgin with the Infant Christ, Elizabeth, the little St. John, Joseph, and two heavenly messengers, or guardian angels, scattering flowers as tokens of their adoration. He also painted 'St. Margaret stepping victoriously upon the Dragon that is coiling round her' (it is much effaced and re-touched); and the portrait of the famous beauty, 'Johanna of Arragon,' the wife of Ascanio Colonna, Prince of Tagliacozzo. From the letters of Beltrame Costabili, Bishop of Adria, the Ferrarese ambassador in Rome from 1516 to 1519, edited by Campore,* we see that originally the Pope had given Raphael the commission to paint a St. Michael, and this with the intention 'of presenting it to his most Christian Majesty of France;' and that the large 'Holy Family' also had been ordered by Leo X., not, however, for Francis I., but for his queen. They were, nevertheless, not presented by the Pope himself, but by Lorenzo de' Medici, Duke of Urbino, who received the pictures, and transmitted them to the French court, despatching them from Florence on June 4, 1518.† Raphael worked at the 'Michael' from March 21, 1517, to May 27, 1518. The 'Johanna of Arragon' was sketched in Naples by a pupil of Raphael's, probably by Giulio Romano, by order of Bernardo Divizio da Bibbiena, who was the Papal legate in France from 1518 to 1519; the greater part of it was executed in oils by Giulio Romano;

* See Appendix, note clxvi. † Ibid. note clxvii.

Francis I. probably received the picture as a present from his legate. Vasari says that Raphael only painted the head, and that all the rest was by Giulio Romano.*

Besides the four last-mentioned pictures, the Louvre Gallery possesses another small 'Holy Family' by Raphael, in which the Infant Christ, standing in the cradle by the side of the Virgin, who is seated, strokes the face of the little St. John, who is sitting on Elizabeth's knee. According to Félibien,† it was painted for the Cardinal Adrien Goffier de Boissi, who was sent to Paris in 1519 as Papal legate. There is no doubt that Giulio Romano and Francesco Penni had a large share in its execution. A second 'St. Margaret,' stepping forth from the rocky cavern, and holding in her left hand a small crucifix, with her eye turned to the dragon, is now in the gallery of the Belvedere at Vienna, after having been for a long time in Venice. The hand of Giulio Romano is here also not to be mistaken; he must also have had an essential share in the design.‡

Many other paintings produced at that time, espe-

---

* See Appendix, note clxviii.   † Ibid. note clxix.
‡ Ibid. note clxx.

cially many Holy Families, can have gone forth from Raphael's atelier alone, although doubtless the master himself had a share in some manner in the conception of all these pictures. Among them we may enumerate the 'Madonna with the Candelabra,' formerly in Lucca, and now in London, in Mr. Munro's collection; the 'Sacra Familia llamada de la Rosa,' now in Madrid, in which the Infant Christ and St. John are holding a parchment scroll with the inscription 'Ecce Agnus Dei;' the 'Holy Virgin among the Ruins,' now in the sacristy of the Escurial; the 'Madonna del Passeggio,' in London (in the possession of Lord Ellesmere); the 'Holy Virgin in the Meadow, with the Infant Christ and St. John,' in the gallery of the Hermitage at St. Petersburg; and others.

The last Madonna which Raphael painted is also his noblest: it is that of San Sisto, in which she is represented with St. Sixtus and St. Barbara. The picture is nine feet three inches high, and seven feet broad, and was, according to Rumohr's supposition,* originally painted on canvass for the monks of the Monastery Church of St. Sixtus, in Piacenza, as a

---

* See Appendix, note clxxi.

drapellone—that is, a procession standard carried between two poles; at all events, however, as Vasari testifies,* it was early placed as a chief altar-piece in the church itself, and in the year 1753 it was purchased for the Dresden Gallery by the Elector Augustus III. of Saxony, for 40,000 scudi romani, with an old copy by the Venetian Nogari.†

The state of the picture is satisfactory, although it has suffered various injuries from accidents, dryness, and the cleaning process of the Roman restorer Palmaroli, in the year 1827. How far it justifies the public opinion that it is the work in which Raphael's genius is most directly exhibited, has never been called in question, except by Count Lepel, who, in his summary of the paintings of Raphael, does not even wish to recognise it as a Raphael picture, and blames its composition and colouring.‡ He has been most convincingly answered by Herr von Quandt.§ Among the various fates which this work of art has experienced, it is especially worthy of remark that Napoleon never carried it away to Paris.

A feeling of spirituality is breathed forth from this

---

* See Appendix, note clxxii.　　† Ibid. note clxxiii.
‡ Ibid. note clxxiv.　　§ Ibid. note clxxv.

picture, a sublimity touching the marvellous, which no other work by our master has attained to an equal extent. It appears the more extraordinary, because a clearer and more simple example of symmetrical and pyramidal arrangement can scarcely be shown in the whole history of the art.* The composition is distinguished by the greatest eurythmy, although the old architectural rule of symmetry prevails to the utmost, and the pyramidal form belonging to the representation of transcendental subjects is employed in the highest simplicity. But not only do pyramidal form and symmetry combine here to produce the utmost artistic freedom, but we see the *sectio aurea* also—a term which the ancients used to denote that just proportion of division by which a given whole (A) is so divided into two parts, that the greater part (B) is the mean proportion between the whole and the lesser part (A—B), or that the whole bears the same proportion to the greater part as this does to the lesser. Although mathematical divisions and figures cannot be called beautiful, and the geometrical arrangement of a picture is opposed to its freedom and picturesque con-

* See Appendix, note clxxvi.

ception—although, moreover, there is no doubt that Raphael did not create the ' Sistine Madonna' according to any dry mathematical plan, previously devised, but in obedience to the inspiration of his own artistic feeling—yet the undeniable fact holds good that in this work there is a wonderful union of geometrical plan with genuine artistic freedom, that the mathematical proportions in it appear resolved into the most perfect harmony, thus affording a new proof that artistic gifts are truly an unconscious science, and that great genius really contains within itself the laws of its art, and exercises them unconsciously. The high importance of symmetry and pyramidal arrangement was well known to our master, and had been for many centuries a matter of artistic teaching. Many of Raphael's paintings prove that he made use of it with full theoretic knowledge, carrying, as he did, the larger pyramidal group into smaller and smaller ones, until at last even the separate figures partook of the same outline. Still, as regards the *sectio aurea*, the knowledge of this just proportion of division, in its application to works of art, may have been foreign to him, although in all classical buildings the proportions of the *sectio aurea* essentially determine the arrangement;

and, from mere imitation of nature, it exists also in figures executed by the sculptor or painter, just as in the human form the principal parts bear this proportion to each other. Notwithstanding this possible ignorance, however, his genius must have felt the infinite harmony of the proportions thus produced; for in him, as in every great artist, we see revealed somewhat of that creative spirit of nature whose proportions submit to the same laws as those which regulate a work of art.*

We will now proceed to point out some details in the 'Sistine Madonna,' without in any wise intending to offer a complete *résumé* of its beauties. The principal thing deserving notice seems to be the powerful effect which our master has thrown into the expression of the eyes. Vischer thus expresses himself on this point:†
' In the " Sistine Madonna," the dark greenish rings of shadow round the eye, and the indescribable treatment of this part, though effected by the simplest means, give a sweet, wonderful, heavenly delicacy to the countenances, which yet breathe forth an existence humanly healthy; hovering down from the realms of heaven to the saints who are imploring protection for

---

* See Appendix, note clxxvii.   † Ibid. note clxxviii.

their church on earth, they seem as if they were saying : No earthly name can designate, no lip can utter, the glorious things we see ; our earthly part is consumed, and yet it lives and moves in the wonders of glory.'

Heinrich Ernst Heucking,* the latest interpreter of this famous work, amid many abstruse and unnecessary discussions, has with some elegance drawn attention to the fact that the treatment 'of the Infant Christ in this picture—with his reserved and satisfied air of independence, with that expression of contemplation which seems like a glance into the future, with his hair fluttering and carried about more by emotions within than by any current of air without, with his bold protruding eye, impatiently distended nostrils, and the almost angrily compressed lips—is just as peculiar, and just as diverse from all other representations of the same subject, as is that of the Virgin, in whom we see, not so much the Queen of Heaven, but the loving afflicted mother, whose sublime expression of melancholy is intended to express how deeply she feels that the possession of the supernatural must bring with it

---

* See Appendix, note clxxix.

unwonted pain, and that martyrdom is the heritage of the great upon earth. Heucking also justly points out the meditative and truth-reflecting glance into the infinite, which wonderfully distinguishes the two careless and innocent boy-angels on the lower edge of the picture from all similar representations by the master. Moritz Carrière * certainly does not err when, criticising Heucking's work, he asserts that, of all Raphael's representations of the Infant Saviour, that in the 'Sistine Madonna' alone portrays the totality of his character and life, the secret of the ideal; that the complete picture of the Man Christ has never been so perfectly executed as in this child—neither by Michael Angelo, who portrayed alone the might of the world-judging Christ without His beneficent tenderness, nor by Titian, nor by Leonardo da Vinci, who, in their pictures of Christ, merely depicted something humanly noble, purity of mind, and loving self-sacrifice, but never to an equal extent represented Him that overcometh the world; nor by Dürer, who, in the title of the ' Great Passion,' exhibits the suffering Redeemer in His agony of soul at the continued sins of mankind;

* See Appendix, note clxxx.

nor, lastly, by Raphael himself, whose ʻTransfiguration͗ portrays alone the *glorified* Christ, though this, too, is executed with the greatest excellence. That a second Virgin like the Sistine has ever again been painted, it would be also difficult to dispute ; analogies alone with the figures of St. Barbara and Pope Sixtus are to be found in other works by the master.

There is one point more to which I must draw attention, and which, in my personal contemplation of the picture, has always appeared to me especially striking, and that is the touching and genuinely human family resemblance seen in the countenance of the Virgin and her Child, which does not, however, in the least affect the utter difference in the spiritual expression of both heads. The face of the mother breathes forth the deepest humblest modesty; that of the child, on the other hand, nothing but energy and animation.

The principal reason why this painting stands so extraordinarily above all the other pictures of this period bearing Raphael's name, refuting so strikingly, as it does, the ridiculous assertion that Raphael retrograded latterly in his art, seems to me to lie in the fact that it was decidedly painted entirely by Raphael himself, without the assistance of his pupils, and this only rarely occurred in the latter years of his life, owing to the multiplicity of his employments. When Palmaroli cleaned the picture, and unsparingly used the knife, some of the colour peeling off, a drawing of the outline in red chalk was distinctly visible; and Rumohr justly supposes that there never was any other sketch but this. In such a case, the 'Sistine Madonna' would be a completely original production of Raphael's genius, in the same manner as the overture to 'Don Juan' is that of Mozart's; for of it, also, not the slightest sketch exists, and the master scarcely effaced a note in first writing it down. Neither the 'St. John the Baptist' as a youth, with a panther-skin on his arm and thighs, sitting by a fountain in the desert—a picture painted for the Cardinal Colonna, and now in the Uffizi at Florence—neither this painting nor Raphael's last work, which was only completed after his death, the 'Transfiguration or Glorification of Christ,' are equal to the 'Sistine Madonna' as regards execution; for they were certainly not entirely finished by the master's own hand. The 'Transfiguration of Christ' (a picture twelve feet six inches high, and eight feet eight inches wide) was painted by order of the Cardinal Giulio de' Medici as an altar-piece for his bishopric of Narbonne. In the year 1522 it was placed as an altar-piece in the church of San Pietro in Montorio; in 1797 it was carried to Paris; and since the year 1815, it has been in the Vatican picture gallery. In this picture, we can only recognise Raphael's brush with certainty in the figure of our Saviour, in the demoniac boy, in the anxious father imploring the assistance of Christ, in the splendid female figure kneeling in the foreground, pointing to the boy, and in the Apostle Andrew, who is sitting to the left. Giulio Romano executed many of the heads of the Apostles, and the lower groups, in a somewhat coarse style; and he also evidently had no unessential share in the figure of St. John the Baptist. Göthe has, however, in his ' Italienische Reise,' for ever thoroughly refuted the blame so often heard respecting the double subject of the ' Transfiguration,' and the lack of connection between the lower and upper portions of the painting. ' It is marvellous,' he writes,* ' that any one should ever have ventured to criticise the great unity of such a conception. In the Saviour's absence, some unhappy parents bring a demoniac boy

* See Appendix, note clxxxi.

N

to the disciples of the Lord : they may already have
attempted to cast out the evil spirit ; a book even has
been opened, to enquire if any traditional form can be
found effective against the evil possession ; but in vain.
At .this moment the only Mighty One appears, and
this in a glorified state, acknowledged by his great
Father.   At once they point to such a vision as to
the one source of safety.   How can one desire to separate the two parts ?   Both are one : below, the suffering, the needy ; above, the Able, the Helper : both
related to each other, both linked together.   And, to
express our meaning in another manner, can an ideal
reference to the actual interfere with this ?   Raphael
was even distinguished for the correctness of his mode
of thinking ; and shall the God-inspired man, whom
we throughout recognise as such, have thought, have
acted falsely, in the very prime of his life?   Nay ;
like Nature, he is at all times right and just ; there
most profoundly so, where we least understand her.'

While alluding to Göthe's efforts to promote an
understanding of Raphael's works, I will not omit to
mention the detailed description of his designs of
' Christ and the Twelve Apostles,' which were engraved
by Marc Anton, and were copied by Langer in Düs-

seldorf in 1789. These designs were painted life-size in succession, on the pillars of the nave of the little church of San Vincenzo ed Anastasio, built in the seventh century, and standing before the Porta San Paolo in Rome, not far from San Paolo fuori le mura; they have now almost entirely disappeared. 'The task,' says Göthe,[*] 'of properly representing a glorified Teacher and his twelve first and chiefest disciples, men who hung entirely on his words and life, and for the most part crowned their simple walk with a martyr's death, has been performed by Raphael with such a complete understanding of art, that we may consider these sheets as the finest monuments of his successful career.' In the 'Italienische Reise' also, we find some more beautiful remarks upon this work of Raphael's.[†] 'This extraordinary mind,' he here says, 'which had before represented these pious men in an assembled band all harmonising in their dress, has pourtrayed them here, where each appears separately, each with his especial and distinctive mark, not as though he were in his Master's train, but as if, after that Master's ascension, he had now to work and endure to

---

[*] See Appendix, note clxxxii.   [†] See Appendix, note clxxxiii.

the end according to his character.' In the management of the drapery especially, an extraordinary art is displayed, and this is pointed out in greater detail in the criticism of Göthe's which we first mentioned.

I must refrain from entering further upon the endlessly manifold designs of Raphael; Passavant has enumerated them most completely. I will only in conclusion refer to one oil-painting, which the master probably left behind him in a most unfinished state. It is ' The Coronation of the Virgin,' which he promised as an altar-piece to the nuns of Monte Luce at Perugia as early as 1505, a promise he again repeated in 1516. The painting was not completed till 1525, when it was executed by Giulio Romano in conjunction with Giovanni Francesco Penni and Berto di Giovanni; the first painted the upper part, where Christ is crowning the Holy Virgin; the second painted the lower part, with the Apostles at Mary's sepulchre; and the third painted the predella, with four representations from the life of the Virgin. This predella has been preserved in the sacristy of the monastery of Monte Luce to the present day. The altar-piece itself was carried in 1797 to the Musée Napoléon, and in 1815 was conveyed to the Vatican.

It now only remains for us to say a few words on
the close of Raphael's career. Whether, as Vasari
thinks,* he met with the early death which we deplore,
in consequence of sensual excesses and the misapplied
remedy of bleeding, or whether, as others assert, he
was carried off by a violent feverish cold, which he
caught while engaged in his excavations and survey-
ings in the old city,† seems to me a question scarcely
worth the trouble which Longhena and Pungileoni
have expended on its solution. That he loved women
is an established fact, even if Vasari in his biography
may have attended too much to the gossiping stories
of contemporaries, when he says: 'Fu Raffaello per-
sona molto amorosa ed affezionata alle donne, e di
continuo presto ai servigi loro.' ‡ If, however, it can
be proved, that according to the general custom of his
time and country, he indulged in amours, and perhaps
a long and intimate intercourse with one beautiful
woman especially, even this does not establish the
fact that mere common sensuality was the cause of
his death; indeed this can scarcely be supposed when
we consider the ideal tendency of his nature, and his

* See Appendix, note clxxxiv.   † See Appendix, note clxxxv.
‡ See Appendix, note clxxxvi.

truly enormous artistic activity up to the very last moment. That his frame of body was delicate is a settled fact; we cannot therefore be surprised that the incessant mental exertions, to which the unwearied artist exposed this tender frame, must have shattered it in the first violent attack of illness. Moreover, the before-mentioned Modenese records, the latest documents relating to his life, confirm the fact that a severe attack of fever carried him off after an illness of eight days.* Pauluzzo, the Roman agent of Duke Alfonso of Ferrara, to whom Raphael had promised a picture, a promise of which he was in vain reminded to the day of his death, expressly informs his master of this circumstance. The artist died at the age of thirty-seven, on the anniversary of the day of his birth, Good Friday, April 6, 1520, between nine and ten o'clock in the evening. He had, however, had time to make his will, appointing as its executors Baldassare Turini da Pescia, secretary to the papal datary, and the papal chamberlain, Giovanni Battista Branconio of Aquila. He had himself chosen the place of his interment in the Pantheon of Agrippa, which was consecrated by Pope Boniface IV. as the church of Santa Maria ad

* See Appendix, note clxxxvii.

Martyres, or della Rotonda, and he had arranged that over his sepulchre a marble statue of the Virgin should be erected, the execution of which he had consigned to Lorenzo Lotti (Lorenzetto). Giulio Pippi (Romano) and Francesco Penni inherited all he possessed in treasures of art, even his still unfinished works; he provided handsomely for the so-called Fornarina. Bibbiena received, as we have before seen, his house in Rome; his relatives in Urbino were the principal inheritors of the rest of his property, with the exception of that on his father's side, which Giovanni Santi had bequeathed to the fraternity of Santa Maria della Misericordia. Besides this, he allotted one thousand scudi for the purchase of a house, from the revenue of which twelve masses for his soul were to be celebrated monthly on the altar of the burial chapel he had founded; these, however, have been discontinued since the year 1705, because the house 'l' Imagine,' in the Via de' Coronari, brings in now but a rent of a few scudi.

The sorrow for Raphael's death was universal. The people of Rome poured forth in crowds to the house of death, where the corpse of the great master was laid out on a catafalco, surrounded with wax torches; behind it stood the painting of the 'Transfiguration.'

Grand was the ceremony of his interment; every artist followed; no eye was tearless, as Vasari says : ' Non fu nessuno artefice che dolendosi non piagnesse, ed insieme alla sepoltura non l' accompagnasse.' * Bembo wrote a Latin epitaph, which may be translated as follows :—

DEDICATED TO
RAPHAEL SANTI, THE SON OF JOHN OF URBINO,
THE GREAT PAINTER WHO EMULATED THE ANCIENTS,
IN WHOSE LIVING WORKS
THE LINK BETWEEN NATURE AND ART
IS EASILY PERCEIVED.
PAINTER AND ARCHITECT, HE INCREASED THE FAME OF POPE JULIUS
THE SECOND AND LEO THE TENTH.
HE LIVED EXACTLY THIRTY-SEVEN YEARS,
AND DIED ON THE ANNIVERSARY OF HIS BIRTH,
ON APRIL 7, 1520.
THIS IS THAT RAPHAEL, BY WHOM NATURE FEARED TO BE
CONQUERED WHILE HE LIVED, AND TO DIE WHEN HE DIED.

•

D. O. M.
RAPHAEL SANCTIO JOHAN. F. VRBINATI
PICTORI EMINENTISS. VETERVMQ. AEMVLO,
CVIVS SPIRANTEIS PROPE IMAGINEIS
SI CONTEMPLERE,
NATURAE ATQVE ARTIS FOEDVS
FACILE INSPEXERIS.
JULII II. ET LEONIS X. PONT. MAX.
PICTVRAE ET ARCHITECT. OPERIBUS
GLORIAM AUXIT.
VIXIT AN. XXXVII. INTEGER INTEGROS.
QUO DIE NATIS EST EO ESSE DESIIT,
VII. ID. APRIL. MDXX.
IILLE HIC EST RAPHAEL, TIMUIT QUO SOSPITE VINCI
RERUM MAGNA PARENS ET MORIENTE MORI.

* See Appendix, note clxxxviii.

The authentic information we possess respecting Raphael's death, is from a letter addressed to Antonio di Marsilio, in Venice, five days after the sad event, on April 11, 1520, from the nobleman Marc Antonio Michiel de Ser Vittor, then living in Rome. It was first published in the 'Notizia d'Opere di Disegno da un Anonimo, etc., da Jacopo Morelli' (Bassano, 1800), page 210, note 128.* In this paper, the whole of the great master's bequest was estimated at 16,000 ducats, which was certainly no small sum at that period. It is also here narrated that the death of Raphael was announced to the Pope by the threatened fall of that part of the Vatican palace which had been built by the artist, and in which Leo X. now lived, so that the prince of the Church was obliged to remove to other apartments (those of the Monsignore Cibo). A great number of poets wrote verses on his death, and Ariosto composed a Latin distich. Among the most touching words written on his mournful decease, are the few lines which Count Castiglione addressed to his mother from Rome on July 20, 1520: 'Io sono sano, ma non pare essere in Roma, perché non vi è più il mio pove-

---

* See Appendix, note clxxxix.

retto Raffaello. Che Dio abbia quell' anima bene-
detta!' (I am well, but it seems no longer as if I
were in Rome, for my poor Raphael is no longer here.
May God have taken him to Himself!) Upon the
disinterment, suggested by the sculptor Fabris, on
September 14, 1833, Raphael's body was found in a
state of tolerable preservation, exactly in the place
specified by Vasari,* that is, in a brick vault under
the chief altar to the left of the entrance. The
skeleton measured five feet two inches, according to
Parisian measure.

* See Appendix, note cxc.

CHAPTER VI.

CONCLUDING REMARKS.

I SHOULD here have brought my sketch of Raphael's life to a close, if I had not felt impelled in conclusion to enter more particularly upon *one* point, which has indeed been often mentioned in the course of my narrative, but which seems to me so exceedingly important in arriving at an understanding of the great man, that I cannot forbear stating once more with greater detail and connection all that perhaps can be said on the subject. I allude, namely, to the peculiar blending of pagan classic lore and Christian romanticism, which was perfected in Raphael's art.

All forms of art, the plastic, painting, poetry, and music, have their distinct epochs, in which they become the centre of man's progressive existence; they then attain their culminating point, and, so to speak, having finished their career, they make room for other forms of art; they depend on certain configurations of mental and civilised life, the adequate expression of which is given in this very art. In the beginning of the sixteenth century, painting thus played its over-ruling part. Raphael raised it to its height, for all preceding artistic efforts converge, to a certain extent, in this master. After him, however, in spite of many very important successors, its decline commenced—an evident proof that the centre of the mental life then dawning, no longer lay in this art.

How was it, however, that just in the first half of the sixteenth century, painting should have occupied such a central position, and have displayed its highest perfection in Raphael?

There were essentially two great mental influences which exerted a power over art previous to Raphael's time;—that of Christianity, which perceives the essence of beauty to lie in the soul and in divine love, hence 'in the light of inspiration;'* and that proceeding from the study of antique, where beauty is based on the genius of nature, the essence of all antique art lying ' in the spirit of the living form, or in the idea of the form.'† These two influences, which have been

---

* See Appendix, note cxci.　　　† See Appendix, note cxcii.

long completely sundered, so entirely indeed, that it appears as if the former had utterly overcome the latter, had at the end of the middle ages obtained a kind of equal authority, through the renaissance of antiquity in literature and art. The mutual prevalence, after which the two influences aspired, first displayed itself in the sphere of painting, for the number of universal geniuses which in this art struggled to free themselves from the one-sidedness of the culture of the middle ages, produced a style, which exhibited indeed a relative union of the Christian and the Pagan, of the romantic and the classic influences.

It is true this union was at first only relative, for, as Vischer says,* 'there still remained a more difficult blending to accomplish, that, namely, in which the picturesque style, with all its definiteness, was to pass into this great school of form. Penetrated by the antique, the *plastic* style of painting adopted at the same time as much of the picturesque as was possible. Thus the influence of the antique was reversed in another manner; just as *it* had carried into the pure form of the beautiful, the true and delicate measure of

* See Appendix, note cxcii.

fidelity to nature and individual characteristics, hence
standing forth as an everlasting model, as an everlasting
example and source of reference; so this high style
of Italian painting displayed the absolute extent to
which the plastic style of painting can admit of the
genuine picturesque.   What ancient art is for all
times, this style, which dates its commencement from
the sixteenth century, is to the future yet to be;
another style, the specifically picturesque, always in
danger of losing its proportion, its nobility, and its
firm support, has ever to look up to this pure and
everlasting model; and the spot where its pure godlike
world is enthroned, is Athens, whither every painter
should make his pilgrimage.'

Certain it is, it was a grand moment when this
mutual inter-penetration and, to a certain extent,
separation of the two elements, was accomplished—of
the antique pagan, with its sensual epicurean tendencies, and the Christian and mediæval, with its character of transcendental ideality—elements which,
when disunited, lead to dangerous one-sidedness.
Both needed a deeper purification and renewal, if
intellectual life were not to fall for ever into two
irreconcilable extremes.   But, when this inter-penetra-

ion had once prevailed at least in *one* sphere of art, it was no wonder that this art immediately occupied a central position in civilised life, holding a prominent position in the age as well as in the nation, from which the great art of union proceeded. A truly humanistic view of things must have been the result of this event, and an art must have sprung forth from it, which we may likewise call humanistic, inasmuch as it harmoniously united the ideal demands of Christianity with the realistic requirements of the antique. We must not, however, picture the extraordinary event as though it had suddenly, as it were, fallen from heaven; on the contrary, it required long preparatory struggles in every sphere of activity open to the mind of man, before such a fruit could come to maturity. To understand this, we must once more examine the cleft that separates the two extremes.

The art of the Christian middle ages found its highest motive in that Christian dogma, according to which each individual has attained his destiny only when he quits the life of sense for that life to come, which is the contrast to the world of sense and time. The ideal is by this means removed from the artistic representation, for all forms of sense (and others we have not), appear insufficient and inadequate for its representation. Such representations can, moreover, never in themselves possess their object; they cannot bring men into harmony with themselves, they can only be conceived as intimations of ˙the nothingness of the world, which is to be overcome. With such a condition, how can we imagine the exercise of art possible, especially as regards painting? It has even been asserted that a Christian art was in truth impossible; for when the ideality of Christianity is represented, the form that presents itself to the senses is ever proved to be the right and suitable one, and the transcendental ideality thus becomes a false fiction. A similar turn of thought, if not quite so absolutely strict, befel in the middle of the fifteenth century the antique pagan school, arising from the revival of the study of antiquity, and this called forth not merely a realistic, but a material and sensual view of life. Since then the art productions gravitate, as regards form and matter, towards one of the two extreme styles; and equally so are these stamped in the most significant forms and in the most marvellous interminglings on society in general. Thus, for example, we see the wearers of the tiara, the representatives of the crucified on earth, influenced by the most sensual aims; morally and politically those extreme tendencies inter_ sect each other in them. The means which the Papacy employed to assert its authority, are not those of the faith which is to overcome the world, but of the power which the constitutional structure of the States of the Church achieves. Yet in spite of this, there can be no dispute as to the grandeur of the political conception with which a Julius II. worked, essentially laying the foundation of the modern position of the Papacy. The hierarchical system thus obtained its sensible consummation; but with this outward poli- tical power, with this sensible representation of itself, its mediæval idea ceased any longer to exist. Or can we reasonably regard it as anything else than a termination of the Christian-mediæval idea, when Julius II. marched through the breach into the con- quered cities, and enforced with cannons the spiritual principles which he advocated?

The Papacy lost its central position at this moment; henceforth it was for all men nothing but a temporal power, ruling no longer by the mind, but by the sword. There was indeed a time, and this lasting for many centuries, when this *supremacy by mind* was a fact conceded even by the fanatical Protestants. Macaulay describes this epoch and the conditions of that supremacy with great distinctness in the first volume of his 'History of England': 'The childhood of the European nations,' says the great historian, 'was passed under the tutelage of the clergy. The ascendancy of the sacerdotal order was long the ascendancy which naturally and properly belongs to intellectual superiority. The priests, with all their faults, were by far the wisest portion of society. It was, therefore, on the whole, good that they should be respected and obeyed. The encroachments of the ecclesiastical power on the province of the civil power produced much more happiness than misery, while the ecclesiastical power was in the hands of the only class that had studied history, philosophy, and public law, and while the civil power was in the hands of savage chiefs, who could not read their own grants and edicts.

'But a change took place. Knowledge gradually spread among laymen. At the commencement of the sixteenth century, many of them were, in every intellectual attainment, fully equal to the most enlightened of their spiritual pastors. Thenceforward, that dominion which, during the dark ages, had been, in spite of abuses, a legitimate and salutary guardianship, became an unjust and noxious tyranny.'* Little as this historical conception of the political-ecclesiastical process can be generally regarded as just, yet so much may be conceded from any point of view, that the Reformation would never have been able to carry out her principle of the free spontaneity of man, and to maintain it to the present day, if the time had not been ripe for it.

Wholly analogous with this political development was the progress of the life of art. All that the middle ages have afforded of artistic treasure, we owe to the Church. But when the mental horizon of men widened, had art still remained in the exclusive service of the Church, it would have been stiffened into a one-sidedness which must have led to its decline, even before the period of its perfection had been reached. With purifying and improving influence, the re-awakened genius of the antique now stept forth to rescue art from the fetters of mediæval opinions, and thus it gradually attained to that free universality and liberty of mind, which, 'with noble sensual

* See Appendix, note cxciv.

delight and imbued with the feeling of heroic human greatness, no longer disdained to admit the graceful and natural type of the antique,' in conjunction with the immaterial, chaste, and supernatural Madonna, and at last produced that perfect ideal of Italian painting, in contemplating which, even we, children of an age ' which, according to Vischer, can no longer accept the transcendental and mythical conception of things,' of an age which has indeed scarcely nothing more left of the middle ages, and of the ancient world, than its artistic and literary reminiscences—even we are able to forget the subject in its free æsthetic treatment. 'We can even freely admire the pure ecclesiastical works of the great masters, without having anything in common with them or their time, as regards historical belief in the subjects; these have become nothing but the artistic motive. Raphael's Madonnas are types of everlastingly beautiful pure womanhood, chaste maternity, maternal love, and all love; Michael Angelo's "Last Judgment" is the type of eternal justice; we can completely separate from them any question as to the existence of the subjects, as to the possibility of the facts.' *

* See Appendix, note cxcv.

How was it then that it was none other than
Raphael who brought about this blending of the two
styles into the most perfect imaginable harmony, and
conveyed 'the golden contents of the Christian spirit
into the silver vessel of antiquity?'* To such a question
Gruyer's work, 'Raphael et l'Antiquité,' which has
just appeared, affords us the most complete answer.
The union of the Christian spirit with the antique
form,—observable even in the frescoes of the Roman
catacombs in the beginning of the Christian era, in
which Christ sometimes bears the features of Apollo,
and sometimes those of Orpheus, a union for centuries
sought after with eagerness, the barbarian iconoclastic
middle ages not excluded, especially however from the
commencement of the Renaissance school,—this union
was never attained until Raphael came, for ably as all
had struggled for it, some had ventured too much and
others not enough. Leonardo da Vinci never reached
the goal from his too great subtilty of style; Michael
Angelo never reached it, from his excessive knowledge
and adherence to nature; Correggio and Titian failed,
because they indulged in a misuse of colour and

* See Appendix, note cxcvi.

sensual effect. Each of these great masters deviated in his own manner from the antique, however much he sought for it, because with each and all the strict measure and just feeling of the beautiful was wanting. Raphael alone—though perhaps in some points not attaining to the height of the others, though perhaps less rich in knowledge than the two first, and less great in colouring than the two last—Raphael alone understood how to unite the most opposite qualities; he had a more healthy judgment upon the conditions of his art than all the others, he possessed the most accurate knowledge of arrangement and harmony, and he loved truth above all, without ever considering her artistically worthy of representation apart from grace and beauty. His heart was Christian, but at the same time his taste was not inferior to that of the master of the Periclean age. In his numberless designs, especially, he displays his peculiar gift for interpreting nature in the manner of the antique. All his works, his earlier ones not excluded, which were created with any exact knowledge of the antique, seem inspired by its spirit, although the master, ever creative and independent, followed his own personal feeling alone; this feeling pre-existed in him, it was not the antique that ed it first into being; nay, it did not even modify ; it only confirmed it and matured it.

Thus it was, that he alone, whilst all the renaissance round him drew its life from paganism or perished through it, according to its reasonable use or abuse; thus it was that he alone, without for a moment ceasing to be a Christian, was able to re-create, as it were, the immortal works of antiquity.* Not that he copied them, but that, just as Schinkel, three centuries later, achieved in architecture, he did anew what the ancients had done; that is, he sought for the ideal amid the fetters of reality, and found the beautiful without deviating in consequence from the truth. The detractors from his fame may lament as much as they will that he lost his orthodoxy in Rome while contemplating the antique. In all the reminiscences of Anacreon, Theocritus, and Sappho, which meet us in his mythological creations, we can always perceive the prevailing voice of the Christian muse—that infinite ardour, that tenderness of love, that knows no limit, that spiritual element, which the antique never possesses, but which Raphael never renounces. The

* See Appendix, note cxcvii.

excesses of paganism have never defiled his brush; he never takes pleasure in the impure. The story of Psyche was to him not merely a subject for delighting in sensuality; he breathed even into it the spirit of that genuine art which may be one's proper object, because in it lie the impulses to all divine and great things of which human nature is capable. How untrue, moreover, is the reproach that Raphael retrograded after having come in contact with the antique, and that in the 'Disputa' he reached the height of his art! How can we forget that it was after this that he painted the most religious of his pictures—the 'Madonna di Fuligno,' the 'Madonna della Sedia,' the 'Madonna di San Sisto,' the 'Spasimo,' the 'Transfiguration?' In art the ideal is orthodoxy, and, from this point of view, Raphael was the most orthodox of painters to the very end of his life. To compare him with Apelles, who indeed blended too thoroughly the realism of the school of Sicyon with the soft and voluptuous Ionic style, is unjust. Apelles painted the gods but little, and avoided grand subjects; Raphael's art, however, embraced all the most important manifestations of religion, poetry, history, and philosophy, and spreads over all points of this boundless sphere the soft, steady, and invigorating fire of a beneficent genius. Could we build a palace, in which the works of Phidias and Raphael should both find a place, we should perceive that they are the only equal representatives of their ages—that is, of ancient and modern times.*

In the unity produced by Raphael's Greek eye and Christian feeling lies the highest point of the artistic progress of all subsequent times—the bond between supernatural and natural beauty—the equalisation of mind and matter—the ripened fruit of a past, which has cast it aside, and thus at the same time an eternally true and enduring symbol of a later age, which seeks through other means—through reflection, through liberty of belief and independence of mind—to obtain in actual reality an equal harmony between the ideal and the real. It is Raphael's merit to have first fully achieved this great work in the sphere of art. By means of that harmonious disposition of nature which, at the commencement of these considerations, turned our attention to Mozart, and which might with equal right have reminded us of

* See Appendix, note cxcviii.

Göthe also, he embraced with equal devotion the two great fundamental divisions or influences in the history of art and civilisation, and blended objectively in his works those opposite tendencies which were subjectively so closely united in his own character; and so complete is this blending, that, although these works belong sometimes to the antique and sometimes to the Christian element, all differences appear entirely extinguished, and from it there arises a burst of human feeling—the dominant, as it were, of the glorious keynote. But in this Raphael proves himself to have advanced as far beyond the specific-mediæval as the antique world. It was this universality of Raphael's genius which Göthe had in view, when he said of him :* 'He never Grecises, but he feels, thinks, and acts entirely as a Greek; so that we see here the finest talent developed as favourably as it would have been under similar conditions and circumstances in the age of Pericles.' And this is justly followed up by Wilhelm von Schadow in these words :† 'This is the reason why Raphael pleases so universally, because every one finds what he requires in his works. In the greater number

* See Appendix, note cxcix.   † See Appendix, note cc.

of them he satisfied the Christian critic by the suitability of their spirit with the subject, and the heathen critic by the beauty and correctness of the form.'

Thus, then, by the all-penetrating power of his genius, although an Italian and a Catholic, he rose far above all national and religious peculiarities into the atmosphere of pure human feeling, influencing equally the Romanic and the Germanic, the Catholic and the Protestant world. He is the painter of all ages, in so far as by means of his art he represents the perfect unity and harmony of all human effort and desire. Whoever can place himself on this high point of universal influence, must find his own desire symbolically represented in Raphael's creations, and must feel himself so elevated and purified by them, that he involuntarily transfers the sublime artistic perceptions expressed by him into the region of thought and practical reality; for he draws from them the heavenly breath of that pure ideality, which is in truth the highest power in all work—in scientific and practical no less than in artistic.

The contrast to such a universal conception of art as we see realised in Raphael's works, is afforded by those tender, sensitive souls who, frightened by the everlasting struggles of the present, seek a refuge on the other side of this rude and hard reality—who appear exclusively disposed to transcendental views, to an escape from the region of the actual, and to a contemplative life. Such characters represent a direction of mind, the truth and importance of which is manifested only in the full harmony of all mental tendencies, but which, separately considered, from the starting point of universality, must be estimated as a disturbance and aberration of the mental. life. I allude especially to the tendency of a school of painting which, in the early part of our own century, in connection subsequently with the Pre-Raphaelites, formed itself in Rome under the influence of the German Romanticists, and which was designated in ridicule 'the Nazarene.' Overbeck, Veit, Schadow, and those of similar opinions, do not find their ideal in Raphael, in whom the struggle between mind and body is ended, and a glorious harmony is attained. Their aspirations go further back, to those early painters of Italy, unripe but more ecclesiastically fettered, who are distinguished by an especial transcendental fervour, by a tendency 'upwards'—a tendency which was decidedly broken by the appearance of the antique-pagan classic style.

In spite of this, the Nazarenes, resting on Fra Angelico da Fiesole, Perugino, and other earlier mas_ters, have again revived and adopted the transcendental principles, in which reality is only a sad interregnum, and the task of all art-representation is to point to the life beyond. But when created forms are naturally chosen for this representation, this is done only to lead the attention from these to a spiritual purport, for which such a picture was intended only to be the vehicle and imperfect suggestion. In the works, therefore, of the masters we have mentioned, another meaning was always intended to be impressed on the spectator than that represented. It was not the forms, not the historical subject, which had an interest in itself; the aim of the painter was directed solely to that which lay behind these, and even the history of the Old Testament was not represented for the sake of showing in it any direct realisation of the Divine will, but it also served the artist only as a Christian allegory. When Overbeck, for example, pourtrayed the ' Expulsion of Hagar,' he did not intend to represent this, but symbolically, according to St. Paul's interpretation, the children of the Church in contrast to those of the synagogue; when he composed the

Judgment of Solomon,' he allegorised in his, according
to the explanation of the Fathers of the Church, the
contrast between the true Church of Christ and the
adherents of sects.* A transcendental meaning is
inadequate to any reality, and for this reason the latter
never appears in its fulness, never in its harmony of
mind and body, never in its unison of reason and sense.
Hence we may explain the lifeless forms, the want of
reality, the absence of the corporeal among the Nazarenes. They satisfied themselves with the simple
outline—with the intimation of lifeless moving spirits.
The work of art became a hieroglyph, the key to
which lay only in an obstinate dogmatism. Consist-
ently followed out, it would at last have shrivelled
up into an everlasting 'Ecce Homo;' the world
wore always a Good Friday face. An art, however,
which leads to this, is a quenching of the spirit;
aye, even of the Holy Spirit, which ought. to guide
mankind into all truth, and into happy concord with
creation.

And yet there lay a truth in this tendency, in the
impulse to fill up the deficiencies, which a style equally

* See Appendix, note cci.

one-sided, though in another direction, had shortly before left behind. I allude to the modern classic and plastic style of painting—that of Karstens, Wächter, and Koch; designers full of mind and style, but weak colourists—the appropriators of the old myths, and the despisers of the more picturesque material of the middle ages. The Christian Romanticists committed only this error in their contest with these modern pagan painters, that they exaggerated their just æsthetic principles into dogmas, and, instead of satisfying their impulse for the picturesque by seeking the more appropriate material in the history of the middle ages, they asserted its myths to be the only true material, and, according to this, they took its immature style as a lawful model.* They, therefore, never reached the extreme, logically in exact opposition to the modern classics, the extreme of the strictly picturesque; but they arrived at 'a prominence of the æsthetic generally, as a world of licence.' This extreme is conceivable, and we owe to it infinitely much, 'especially in the expression of deep feeling, and something also in animation of colour;'† yet still how far removed is it,

---

* See Appendix, note ccii.   † See Appendix, note cciii.

just because it is an extreme, from that unity and harmony of contrasts attained three hundred years ago.

I have introduced these modern schools into the limits of my remarks, because I thought we might thereby obtain a standard for judging the height at which Raphael stands. If, however, I have pronounced sentence against the modern Christian Romanticists, I have done so merely in the name of that sound universal school of cinque cento, which knew how to employ the transcendental spirit of the middle ages as well as that of the ancient world, in guiding art to its great aim of equalising mind and matter. Certain it is, Raphael was a Christian painter; but if we will embrace the whole infinite genius of this man in the idea of Christianity, we must conceive the latter as vast as it ought to be conceived. The transcendental element in the master's conceptions is of such a kind, that it seems, as it were, vanished to him for whom it has no meaning, or only one of a more limited cha-racter, obscured by reflection, and only that fervour of mind, that tenderness of soul, that depth of feeling, that connection between the mind of the artist and his subject, remains visible, with which the creative spirit rooted itself in his subject, and yet, æsthetically free, hovered above it.*

I cannot sanction the opinion that Raphael himself had no faith in the subjects which he represented, and that it was intentionally that in so many of his pictures of saints (as, for example, the figures of St. Magdalene and St. Barbara in the 'St. Cecilia' and the Sistine 'Madonna') he introduced glances not directed up- wards, but straightforward or downwards—glances, too, which, compared with the other upward-gazing and adoring figures, expressed a profane course of life in all their charms and indifference, as if to oppose to the transcendental enthusiasm and rapture of the others, the unconstrained human acknowledgment: 'We draw our joys from earth.' I consider this view just as false as the opposite one, which we also continually meet with, and which amounts to this, that there is no idea at all of a worldliness of expression in such figures of Raphael's, that they far rather pourtray the specific character of the saint repre- sented in another form indeed, but equally strongly as the other figures. Thus, for example, in the 'St.

* See Appendix, note cciv.

P

Barbara,' according to an article by W. Passauer in
the 'Illustriste Welt,'* the woman is represented
' casting her eyes to the ground in the sense of her own
unworthiness in comparison with the Virgin's self-
sacrifice; the woman who, not born for action, des-
ponds when she herself can offer no sacrifice—bend
ing her knee in humble adoration and full of reverence—the woman who, according to her destiny, finds
satisfaction in the sacrifice and adoration of that which
appears to her an inconceivable act.' Nothing of all
this can I perceive in the 'St. Barbara' as she stands
before me with no halo of glory. I should rather
regard this whole controversy in general as useless,
insignificant, and entirely resting on the old experience,
that art-critics are only too inclined to transfer their
own private opinion to the work of the artist, and to
discover a fresh confirmation of this in each separate
production. Although it is certain that, for example, in
the earlier Sienese and Umbrian schools, figures of such
a worldly exterior as St. Barbara and St. Magdalene
had never been produced, yet Raphael created them assuredly not, as it were, only as a proof of his inward

* See Appendix, note ccv.

unbelieving, anti-ecclesiastical views, as a symbol of a mental reservation, as a self-excuse for his representation of sacred subjects, which possessed nothing of sacredness for him, but far rather because overruled by picturesque reasons, and at the same time in obedience to a certain instinctive feeling, which revealed to him the truth, still often unperceived, that beauty of form has in itself an artistic, aye, even an ethical importance, as the vehicle of the ideal of beauty. That Raphael, even in his representations from sacred history, indulged in such purely artistic motives, is proved by the immense advance he made compared with his predecessors; we are also assured of it when we see how far he outstepped all hitherto dogmatic and ecclesiastical aims in the exercise of his art, and thus gradually made its object the whole unlimited sphere of human life.

Certain it is, that there is not a trace to be discovered in his character of the frivolity of a Voltaire, nor of the scoffing infidelity of modern sceptics and materialists; he *believed*, according to the statutes of his Church, in the Mother of God and in all saints, as much as any of his contemporaries; he was even, indeed, received, on March 1, 1514, into the strict ecclesiastical and Catholic Fraternitas Corporis Christi at Urbino—a fraternity which, originating in Rome and existing, even to the present day, in all the more important cities of Catholic Christendom, pledged its members to an especially active participation in the sacrament of the Eucharist. But when Raphael created his pictures of saints and virgins, he did so as an artist who had been trained in the pagan school as well as in the Christian, and who, above all, limited by no narrow-minded considerations, knew how to draw from the fountain-head of nature with the purest and fullest freedom of mind, recognising, whether the subject to be represented was profane or sacred, no other law than that of beauty, the idea of which was ever present with him. That he was permitted to do this, without giving offence to his patrons, he owed partly to the enlightenment of his age, which, by literary, scientific, and artistic efforts of various kinds, was sufficiently prepared to allow itself to be easily carried away by the new ideal, thus displayed in all its reality; but he owed this permission, for the most part, to his own unattainable genius, which, like every true genius, was strong enough to stand before the world and proclaim: I am myself the lawgiver!

Christianity calls into exercise the feelings of men far

more than antiquity was able to do, and hence, undeniably, mediæval art acquires its peculiar character.
When, therefore, in Raphael this deep feeling is linked
in the utmost harmony with ancient plastic art, he
seems by this means to stand at the turning-point of
two great epochs of civilisation, and is essentially characterised as belonging to a modern age, which labours
continually at a synthesis of the middle ages and antiquity, without having hitherto discovered its principles.
The type of antiquity is the objective form, the plastic;
the type of the middle ages is deep feeling, from
whence our music (originating in church melodies)
arose, as the prime of its perfection. The transition,
however, to modern art, whose most distinguishing
characteristic it is, that, full of thought, it culminates
in poetry and rhetoric, is effected by painting, which
may be defined, therefore, as the musical-plastic art,
because this art, like all mental life, rests on two
fundamental agents, one subjective and one objective—
on the world of feeling on the one side, and on that of
outward things on the other; and because, when these
two agents, each by itself, are artistically perfected,
music and the plastic art arise as the two opposite
poles, within which all other forms of art revolve—

which are, in truth, only various proportions of the blending of these two agents. Architecture derives its significance from the subjective side; it imitates in itself none of the forms of nature, but it has as its foundation the realisation of human objects. These, conceived as the highest points of art, and formed into an ideal harmony, justify the designation of this art as *plastic music*; whilst painting, taking her objects from nature, not, however, in plastic repose, but penetrated and filled with human feelings, representing longing, sadness, rapture, and so forth, may with equal justice be designated as a *musical plastic* art. While painting, however, in undertaking the highest themes in the age of the cinque-centists, and displaying the Ideal, the Eternal, and the Divine, not as the gods of the ancient world, but as sacred pictures produced by religious feeling, formed the transition we have before pointed out,—a part of extraordinary importance belongs to this art in the history of human civilisation. And this is, indeed, in nowise denied her. In the thorough revolution of ideas which she caused in the period of her highest prime, this fact, perhaps, is most worthy of observation, that the *great painter*, Michael Angelo, Raphael's only rival, made the resolution shortly before the close of his career, which he was long ere hé attained, to take leave of art altogether, and to absorb himself entirely in contemplation. We may, of course, perceive in this only an individual caprice; yet involuntarily it acquires a special importance from the fact that it arose in the mind of one of the greatest artists of all ages, and this in the golden period of the art he had especially exercised. We may trace herein a prophetic utterance of the course which art in general was to take—it was to give place to scientific reflection—and thus in modern times to acquire a position totally different to that which it had possessed in the great epoch of which we have been treating—that is, it was to hold a subordinate place. Formerly the centre, it now withdrew aside; formerly the principal thing, it now became ornament and arabesque.

The end of the middle ages, and the beginning of modern times, may be called the classic epoch of painting, because in a certain measure it was the last attempt to reconcile the objective and subjective; but this union falls beyond the domain of the plastic arts, and belongs to that of thought, the key to which may be perceived in the art productions of the time. The plastic arts fell at once into decline, as soon as the word was issued for subjective religious liberty; for in this liberty of thought, life obtains a new centre, and the stars of art recede in the light of this day-star. When, however, Raphael's divine form still walked the earth, painting then stood above all as the highest acquisition to which the Romanic nations had ever attained; the bond between religion and beauty, heaven and earth, was concluded. And yet this glorious prime contained in itself even then the germs of its dissolution. The soul of Italian art perished, when the noble author of that incomparable bond was snatched from earth. Because he had summed up in himself all the perfections of former times, there was now only a fragmentary sundering of his universal aims left behind on the field of art. Raphael forms no school, because he is the end and close of an era in mental development; all that could be expressed within the sphere of art which he embraced, was expressed by him; his pupils are indeed only pupils, who culti-vate his manner. Inadequate imitation, syncretism, and artificial work, this is all that comes after him. Even the most talented imitators of the great style of Raphael and Michael Angelo lack ever something, 'a last touch, a dot to an I, a point of light in an eye;' * and although Titian maintained the high fame of the Venetian school long after Raphael (he did not die till 1576), and this school, on account of its solid and healthy study of nature, declined less rapidly in style than the Roman school, whose decline is observable as early as the middle of the sixteenth century; and although even among the later eclectics, who endeavoured to unite the grace of Correggio with the serious grandeur of the Roman masters, a Guido Reni, who lived till 1642, towers above all as a master of a peculiarly spiritual style of painting; it yet remains evident that neither the later Venetians, nor Guido, nor the contemporaneous Caracci belong to the age of the cinque-centists, in which painting formed the central point of all the mental culture of Italy. The political destinies of Italy interrupted the lasting culture of the spirit excited by Raphael. The living genius of that day grasped with awakened thought after paths essentially new, in which artistic intervention seems only fictitious. The forms of art which appear after this period are essentially those in which thought

* See Appendix, note ccvi.

and reflection hold a distinguished place, so that at last thought appears, so to speak, in *puris naturalibus* in those philosophers, with whom it maintains a principal importance both for science and life.

In this state of things, to remodel life anew and ever to be born again, is the task that lies before the present; it cannot avoid the process, however fruitless it may regard it, and however essentially practical in their character may be its aims for the moment. Art need not therefore be idle; under any circumstances she must co-operate for the highest aims of mankind, while she leads them ever anew to consciousness, and is appointed to beautify and to regulate the structure of human life in all its parts. This must she do, even when she appears more than ever removed from her central position. And who, moreover, would presume to deny her for ever the possibility of once again appearing in the central point of all intellectual life! He who believes in an advance of mankind cannot despair of this possibility; for it is art alone, and not science, nor even industry and multiplication of material, which conquers in those battles of the human mind that form the true epochs of history. Only when the entire life of the man represents a work of art, is it to be called truly happy and morally beautiful, and from such an ideal we are still far distant.

We do not, therefore, lack scope for artistic activity; art has yet indeed a task to achieve. But who can foretell *when* this may be? For the civilisation of the modern Christian era, which begins with Raphael's age, *he* prepared the way; all opposition to our civilisation is extinguished in Raphael's art. We see not indeed the epoch of a still higher art; but the probability of its existence seems as though it might be anticipated as the one encouragement for the future of the human race. Phidias towers above Raphael; for the latter drew his conceptions, like the entire age of the Renaissance, from the antique ideal of beauty, far more than from the works of the later Greek or even Roman art, which even to our own day impedes our unbiassed imitation of Phidias. How much harm has the 'Laocoon' of Michael Angelo done in its classic imitation, how long have we seen the spirit of the antique only through the glasses of a ruder Roman art and literature, how long have we been kept aloof from a deeper study of the Greek tragedies and of Pindar, in whom lies the key to a true understanding of the Periclean-Hellenic art! Even at the present day,

Phidias stands before us as a mystery, whose interpretation we have never reached. Christianity has not yet been brought into harmony with the ideal of Phidias. If, however, it is appointed to us to attain to this, it will be the hand of an artist that accomplishes the work.

No immediate future can possibly produce this artist. Amid the small prospects that remain to us, it only concerns us to guard the possession we have gained against the attacks of extreme tendencies, and to set aside all disturbances thus arising to the unity already attained, in the maintenance of which all human efforts should concur. Wherever this is the case, we shall feel ourselves filled with enthusiasm for Raphael—the first establisher of this unity in the world of art,—as a master homogeneous and kindred with our own time; his importance will endure for all ages, for he was a fellow-labourer in those most important problems of life which are committed to all mankind.

APPENDIX.

NOTE I. Page 5.

Parallel between Rochlitz, Raphael, and Mozart (Allgemeine Musikalische Zeitung, ii. 641, *et seq.*), also between
Alberti, Raphael, and Mozart (Stettin, 1856).

NOTE II. Page 5.

Jahn's Mozart, iv. 744, *et seq.*

NOTE III. Page 5.

Ibid., iv. 746.

NOTE IV. Page 5.

See Schelling's Works (Stuttgart and Augsburg, 1860), vii.
305, *et seq.*, in the paper : Ueber das Verhältniss der
bildenden Künste zu der Natur (1807).

NOTE V. Page 9.

Ibid., p. 318, *et seq.*

NOTE VI. Page 11.

See Friedrich Theodor Vischer's Aesthetik oder Wissen-
schaft des Schonen (Stuttgart, 1853), iii. 3, 716–717.

NOTE VII. Page 14.

Goethe's Works, edition of 1833, xl. 205.

NOTE VIII. Page 15.

Conférences de Notre-Dame de Paris, par le R. P. Henri-Dominique Lacordaire (Paris, 1861), i. 175.

NOTE IX. Page 18.

See Phantasien uber die Kunst. Tieck (Berlin, 1814), new edition, p. 28.

NOTE X. Page 19.

See Guhl, Kunstlerbriefe (Berlin, 1853), i. 113–114.

NOTE XI. Page 19.

See Springer, Raphael's Disputa (Bonn, 1860), p. 3.

NOTE XII. Page 25.

This picture, a Holy Family, has been presented by the painter Wicar to his native city, Lille. Cf. Guhl, Künstler-briefe, i. 121.

NOTE XIII. Page 25.

Cf. Agostino Oldoini with Passavant's Rafael von Urbino und sein Vater Giovanni Santi (Leipsic, 1839–58), i. 521.

NOTE XIV. Page 29.

Cf. Passavant's Rafael, ii. 9–28.

NOTE XV. Page 29.

See Le Vite de' più eccellenti Pittori, Scultori e Architetti di Giorgio Vasari (Triest, 1862), i. 537.

NOTE XVI. Page 30.

See Le Vite, 398, 399.

Note XVII.   Page 30.

That Vasari's statement in the Life of Pinturicchio (pp. 398, 399), a statement which he has himself essentially modi_ fied in his Life of Raphael, p. 537, may be modified into Raphael's share in the Sienese frescoes, is clearly explained by Felix le Monnier in his remarks in the Florentine edition of Vasari (1846). (Cf. Triest edition, from which our quotations are always taken, p. 400, columns 1 and 2, note i., and p. 401, column 1).

The passages alluded to are as follows :—pp. 398, 399, ' Ma è ben vero che gli schizzi e i cartoni di *tutte* le storie ch' egli (Pinturicchio) vi fece, furono di mano di Raffaello da Urbino,' while at p. 537 we read : ' Il quale (Pinturicchio) essendo amico di Raffaello e conoscendolo ottimo disegnatore, lo condusse a Siena, dove Raffaello gli fece *alcuni* disegni e cartoni di quell' opera.'

Note XVIII.   Page 31.

See Quatremère de Quincy, Histoire de la Vie et des Ouvrages de Raphael (2nd edition, Paris, 1838), ii. 37–38.

Note XIX.   Page 32.

This is decidedly an error of Quatremère's. According to Winckelmann, Bötticher, and others, by far the greater number of antiques generally known had been excavated before the end of the sixteenth century.

Note XX.   Page 33.

There is indeed extant in print a letter of recommendation, dated October 1, 1504, from Johanna, the daughter of Federigo of Urbino, and wife of Francesco Maria della Rovere, the prefect of the city of Rome, to the gonfaloniere Pietro Soderini in Florence (Cf. Bottari, Raccolta di Lettere sulla Pittura, Scultura, e Architettura (Rome, 1759–1770), i. 1 ; Pungileoni, Elogio Storico di Raffaello Santi da Urbino (Urbino, 1829), p. 45, *et seq.*; Guhl, Künstlerbriefe, i. 118–119 ; Passavant, i. 527, 528, *et seq*). I, however, share Hermann Grimm's suspicion, that this letter was a subsequent contrivance, and therefore not genuine. (Cf. the paper ' Rafael's Disputa und Schule von Athen, seine Sonette und seine Geliebte,' in the Preussische Jahrbücher, by Haym, Berlin, 1864 vol. xiii. pt. i. pp. 22–24). The following passage appears, for instance, in the letter :—' As his father is a most excellent man and on terms of intimacy with myself, and the son is also modest and well-mannered, I am exceedingly fond of him in every respect, and desire that he should arrive at great perfection.' Giovanni Santi, however, had in 1504 been dead for ten years, and the ' perchè il padre so che è molto virtuoso ed è mio affezionato,' of the Italian text is, therefore, a stumbling-block, which Rumohr endeavours to remove by substituting ' il padre suo stato è,' for ' so che è ; ' while the Florentine editors of Vasari (see p. 537, column 2, note ii., of the Triest edition), suppose that in the manuscript it was written ' so,' that is, the abbreviation for ' suto,' and that Bottari, who first edited the letter, inserted the following ' che ' and the second ' è ' (*che* è molto virtuoso, ed *è* mio affezionato). *Suto* instead of *stato* is, however, only to be found in prose among the Trecentists, and in Raphael's time it was a rare poetic expression. Pungileoni, lastly, is of opinion (pp. 45, 46) that it was not Raphael who was alluded to in the letter, but another painter of Urbino, named Raffaello di Ghisello, who appeared in the middle of the sixteenth century. None of these interpretations please me, and I am therefore inclined to believe in a subsequent invention of the letter, which is not an unusual circumstance in Italian literature.

I must also draw attention here to the following doubt. Quatremère de Quincy, Histoire de Raphael, pp. 18–22, in order to remove pretended errors and anachronisms in Vasari's narrative, gathers together a consecutive account of the events in Raphael's life at that time, partly from the statements of the Vita inedita di Raffaello da Urbino illustrata con note da Angelo Comolli (Rome, 1790, 2nd edition 1791, p. 10, note xvi.), an anonymous work, which is only to be consulted with caution. In 1503, he makes him separate from Siena and Pinturicchio; immediately afterwards he visits Florence for the first time (and this indeed for other reasons than for the sake of the cartoons of Da Vinci and Michael Angelo); after that he resides for a year partly there and partly in Perugia, and towards the end of the year 1504 he returns to Urbino; and then for the second time he goes to Florence for the sake of the cartoons,—this time with Joanna di Rovere's letter of recommendation. These conjectures, however, rest on erroneous premises. Quatremère thinks that Pinturicchio's works in the Libreria at Siena were finished in 1503, that Vasari says in his Vita of Raphael that the latter left Siena for Florence, attracted by the *already completed* cartoons of Da Vinci and Michael Angelo, and that the cartoon of the latter was not finished till July 1506. Vasari's editors, however, show that Pinturicchio was occupied at Siena at all events till 1506, and perhaps even till 1509. (Trieste edition, p. 399, note i., and p. 400, note ii., to the before-mentioned note in the Vita of Pinturicchio.) Raphael, therefore, need not necessarily have gone to Florence as early as 1503, to have left Siena before the completion of the frescoes, and the passage in Vasari's life of Raphael, in which he speaks of the Florentine cartoons (p. 537), reads simply thus: 'La cagione che egli non continuò (quell' opera a Siena) fu, che essendo in Siena da alcuni pittori con grandissimi lodi celebrato il cartone che Lionardo da Vinci aveva fatto nella sala del papa in Fiorenza d' un gruppo di cavalli bellissimo per farlo nella sala del palazzo, e similmente alcuni nudi fatti, a concorrenza di Lionardo, da Michelagnolo Buonarotti molto migliori, venne in tanto desiderio Raffaello per l' amore che portò sempre all' eccellenza dell' arte che . . . . se ne venne a Fiorenza.' Where is there one word here saying that Michael Angelo's cartoon was already completed, when Raphael went to Florence? Vasari says nothing further than that Lionardo at that time had completed (aveva fatto) his cartoon in competition with Michael Angelo, who had executed some nude forms of extreme beauty. The cartoon of Michael Angelo was, on the other hand, according to Gaye, Carteggio inedito d' Artisti dei Secoli XIV.–XVI. (Florence, 1840), ii. 92–93, completely finished by August 1505. (Cf. p. 1041, note i., of the Vita di Michelagnolo by Vasari.) The uncritical and conjectural nature of Quatremère's history is sufficiently evidenced by this one example.

Note XXI. Page 35.

Cf. Kugler, Handbuch der Kunstgeschichte (3rd edition, Stuttgart, 1859), vol. ii. pt. ii. p. 626.

Note XXII. Page 36.

Braun, Raffael's Disputa (Düsseldorf, 1859), p. 57.

Note XXIII. Page 36.

See Le Vite, p. 557.

Note XXIV. Page 37.

Vischer, Aesthetik (Reutlingen and Leipsic, 1851), pt. iii. section i. p. 129.

Note XXV. Page 39.

See Passavant, Kunstreise durch England und Belgien (Frankfort on the Maine, 1833), p. 99.

Note XXVI. Page 39.

See Passavant's Rafael, i. 87, ii. 38. It is not in the Pinakothek.

Note XXVII. Page 41.

See Passavant's Kunstreise durch England, p. 173–4.

Note XXVIII. Page 41.

Ibid., p. 148.

Note XXIX. Page 41.

See Le Vite, in the Vita di Baccio d' Agnolo, p. 722.

Note XXX. Page 42.

A circular picture, in which the Virgin is represented at the right, sitting in a country scene, holding the Infant Christ, wrapt round with one end of her veil, while on the left, Joseph, kneeling, is offering him flowers, towards which he holds out both his hands. This picture is, unfortunately, in a very bad condition, not only very much stained, but also much effaced; it was transferred from wood to coarse canvass.

The figure of Joseph, moreover, appears to be by another hand. Cf. Passavant, Kunstreise durch England, p. 53.

Note XXXI. Page 43.

This brilliant court is accurately depicted in Giesebrecht's and Böhmer's periodical, Damaris (Stettin, 1864), vol. iv. No. i. p. 49 *et seq.*, entitled 'Der Fürstenhof der letzten Montefeltri in Urbino,' by Giesebrecht.

Note XXXII. Page 43.

Castiglione, Poesie Volgare e Latine (Rome, 1760), xxi.

Note XXXIII. Page 46.

See Passavant, Kunstreise durch England und Belgien, p. 103–104, and Giesebrecht, Damaris (1864), p. 62.

Note XXXIV. Page 46.

Le Vite, p. 539.

Note XXXV. Page 46.

Cf. Ernst Förster's paper in the Deutschen Museum (1864), No. xix. p. 691, entitled 'Die Pinakothek in München.'

Note XXXVI. Page 47.

See Passavant's Life of Raphael, ii. 73.

Note XXXVII. Page 48.

Histoire de Raphael, p. 46.

Note XXXVIII. Page 48.

Le Vite, p. 540.

Note XXXIX. Page 49.

Förster considers it to have been painted immediately before the above-mentioned 'Holy Family' of D. Canigiani, which the picture certainly resembles in colouring. The period at which the 'Madonna dei Tempi' was executed is not indeed accurately certain; but it is allowed, as Förster shows, that in composition and execution it is superior to the picture painted for Canigiani, though, on the other hand, the 'Madonna dei Tempi' possesses far more of Perugino's feeling than that painting.

Note XL. Page 50.

See Passavant, Kunstreise durch England und Belgien, p. 99.

Note XLI. Page 53.

See Rumohr, Ueber Rafael, pp. 75, 76.

Note XLII. Page 53.

Gothe's works (edition of 1840), xxx. 466–467. See the paper entitled 'Antik und Modern.'

Note XLIII. Page 55.

Passavant, Rafael, i. 135.

Note XLIV. Page 56.

Gühl, Künstlerbriefe, i. 113.

Note XLV. Page 56.

See Herman Grimm's paper upon Raphael in the Preussische Jahrbücher, January 1864, p. 35.

Note XLVI. Page 57.

Richardson, Traité de la Peinture (Amsterdam, 1722), iii. p. 323. ' J'ai un ami qui a vu à Rome . . . une lettre originale de Raphael à Arioste (which has been lost) dont le contenu consistait à lui demander son secours pour le tableau de " La Théologie," par rapport aux caractères des personnes qu'il devait y faire entrer,' &c.

Note XLVII. Page 58.

This designation did not proceed, as in the other Vatican apartments, from the choice of the pictures, but from the business executed here. Cf. Bangen, Die römische Curie (Münster, 1854), pp. 370 and 391.

Note XLVIII. Page 58.

Cf. Springer, Disputa, pp. 6–7.

Note XLIX. Page 60.

See Rumohr, pp. 85, 86, 97.

Note L. Page 60.

Bellori, Descrizione delle Immagini dipinte da Raffaello nelle camere del Vaticano (Rome, 1695).

Note LI. Page 60.

Trendelenburg, Raphael's School of Athens (Berlin, 1843).

Note LII. Page 60.

Le Vite, pp. 542–543.

Note LIII. Page 61.

Cf. Preussische Jahrbücher, January 1864, pp. 32–33.

Note LIV. Page 61.

Braun, Raphael's Disputa, p. 67.

Note LV. Page 63.

Cf. Preussische Jahrbücher, January 1864, p. 28.

Note LVI. Page 65.

Springer, Disputa, pp. 42–43 ; and Preussische Jahrbücher, January 1864, p. 36.

Note LVII. Page 65.

Springer, Disputa, pp. 23, 26, and 27.

Note LVIII. Page 66.

Preussische Jahrbücher, January 1864, p. 37.

Note LIX. Page 67.

Le Vite, p. 541.

Note LX. Page 67.

' That the titles Timeo and Etica, even if the books formerly bore these inscriptions, are modern in their present form, can scarcely be a matter of dispute. They would hardly have been permitted in Raphael's time in such orthography in such a place. According to Vasari's statement, however, they have only been applied by moderns.'—Cf. Grimm, in the Preussische Jahrbucher, February 1864, pp. 152–153.

NOTE LXI.   Page 70.

See Preussische Jahrbücher, January 1864, pp. 32–33.

NOTE LXII.   Page 73.

Cf. Herman Grimm's paper in the Preussische Jahrbücher, February 1864, pp. 150–153, where all the reasons
are put together, which are in favour of the supposition that
Paul, and not Plato, is represented.   When Grimm, in conclusion (p. 159), with perhaps an exaggerated consideration
for Vasari, begins again to doubt respecting Paul, I do not
feel inclined to follow his scruples.   Raphael may have
heaped anachronism on anachronism in the ' School of Athens,'
and thus have given occasion for the many erroneous interpretations which this picture has suffered; in the idea itself,
on which the dramatic interest of the whole conception
depends, and which invests it with true unity 'and power,
there is certainly no obscurity, and this idea comes before us
with perfect clearness, and superior to all anachronisms, when
we see St. Paul, the great apostle of the Gentiles, by the side
of Aristotle, the representative of scholastic theology.   The
more we fulfil our duty of interpreting the conceptions of
the great masters of the golden age only by the opinions of
their own time, not approaching their works with the measur-
ing scale of modern critics, the more certainly, in spite of
Vasari, though a contemporary, do Paul and Aristotle stand
their ground.   All that we dislike in this interpretation
may be put down to a naïve caprice and custom prevailing
in all the pictures of this period, and which indeed does not
in the least affect their *artistic* perfection.   Think, for
example, of the portraits in the pictures of the Madonna and
Saints of the fifteenth and sixteenth centuries.   It is no

historical, but an artistic truth which they reveal. One more
curious fact yet remains to be mentioned. In Thomassin's
engraving of the ' School of Athens,' in the year 1617, the
two central figures are adorned with a halo, from which it
appears that the Apostle Peter was at that time recognised in
Aristotle ; but this interpretation, as Springer shows (Disputa,
p. 9), evidently belongs entirely to an age in which humanistic'
studies had fallen into oblivion in Rome and Italy, a stricter
church discipline had again prevailed, and in consequence of
this the apotheosis of the Greek genius depicted in the ' School
of Athens ' was no longer understood. At that time the interpreters changed the purport of the picture into a dispute of
the two princes of the apostles with Greek philosophers; but
this interpretation certainly does not belong to Raphael's
time.

Note LXIII.   Page 73.

Cf. Grimm, Preussische Jahrbücher, January 1864, p. 36.
Grimm is certainly right when, in opposition to Vasari's
editors, he considers the ' Parnassus ' to have been painted
before the ' Disputa ' and the ' School of Athens,' and the date
1511, which stands below it, and which the other pictures
lack, to refer to the completion of the whole apartment, and
not to this especial painting. Vasari himself considers the
' School of Athens ' to have been the first and the ' Disputa '
the last of the three compositions.

Note LXIV.   Page 75.

Cf. Europa, a periodical edited by F. v. Schlegel, vol. i. pt. i.
p. 114. ' There is no confusion of men, but few and separate
figures, completed with that care which is natural to a sense

of the dignity and sacredness of the sublimest of all hiero-
glyphic problems—namely, human life.'

Note LXV.   Page 75.

See Lanzi, Storia Pittorica, ii. 58.

Note LXVI.   Page 75.

See Roscoe's Life of Leo X., iii. 240.

Note LXVII.   Page 77.

See Vischer, Aesthetik, iii. 1, 23.

Note LXVIII.   Page 77.

Ibid., ii. 498 ; iii. 3, 713.

Note LXIX.   Page 78.

See Gaye, Carteggio•Inedito d' Artisti, ecc., ii. 489.

Note LXX.   Page 80.

Cf. Grimm, Preussische Jahrbücher, February 1864,
pp. 156–157, in which Michael Angelo's indisputable influence
upon Raphael is represented far more dispassionately, and on
far better authority, than is the case with Passavant and with
Rumohr before him, the latter of whom could not with the
same certainty decide the controversy respecting the reasons
for the change in Raphael's style, since he assigned a later
date to Michael Angelo's frescoes in the Sistina. The passage in Vasari's Life of Michael Angelo (Le Vite, p. 1046),
' dove Raffaello da Urbino, che era molto eccellente in
imitare, vistola (namely, the frescoes on the ceiling of the

Sistine chapel), mutò subito maniera,' agrees throughout with the above-quoted account in Gaye's Carteggio.

Note LXXI. Page 80.

See Le Vite, p. 544.

Note LXXII. Page 81.

Quatremère de Quincy, Histoire de la Vie et des Ouvrages de Raphael, p. 77.

Note LXXIII. Page 81.

Cf. Grimm's paper, Preussische Jahrbücher, February 1864, p. 156.

Note LXXIV. Page 82.

Michael Angelo's relation to the antique has been estimated more impartially by Friederichs in Berlin than by Winckelmann. Cf. Christliches Kunstblatt für Kirche, Schule und Haus (Stuttgart, 1864), February 1, No. ii. p. 17 *et seq.*

Note LXXV. Page 82.

Le Vite, pp. 557–558. 'Ma conoscendo che non poteva in questa parte arrivare alla perfezione di Michelagnolo, come uomo di grandissimo giudizio, considerò che la pittura non consiste solamente in fare uomini nudi, ma che ell' ha il campo largo . . . e mescolando col detto modo alcuni scelti delle cose migliori d' altri maestri, fece di molte maniere una sola, che fu poi sempre tenuta sua propria, la quale fu e sarà sempre stimata dagli artefici infinamente.'

Note LXXVI. Page 83.

Lettera di Michelangiolo Buonarotti, trovata da S. Ciampi (Florence, 1834), p. 7.

Note LXXVII. Page 83.

Cf. Essays (Hanover, 1859), pp. 188, 197, 198.

Note LXXVIII. Page 83.

Lomazzo, Idea del Tempio della Pittura (Milan, 1590–4).

Note LXXIX. Page 84.

The same account may be found in M. de Piles' Abrégé de la Vie des Peintres (Amsterdam and Leipsic, 1767 ; vol. i. of the Œuvres Diverses, p. 103); while Quatremère de Quincy, Raphael, p. 339, note iii., changes 'prévôt' into 'générale.'

Note LXXX. Page 85.

Le Vite, p. 562. I have availed myself of Schorn and Förster's translation, vol. iii. sect. i. p. 250.

Note LXXXI. Page 86.

Le Vite, p. 536.

Note LXXXII. Page 86.

Paolo Giovio's Raphaelis Urbinatis Vita first appeared in Girolami Tiraboschi's Storia della Litteratura Italiana (Milan, 1822–1826, vol. xiv.); Passavant has inserted this short Latin sketch of the author, who had been living in Rome in the papal court since the year 1516, in the appendix of his first volume, No. xv. pp. 553–554.

Note LXXXIII.   Page 87.

Le Vite, p. 562.

Note LXXXIV.   Page 87.

Grimm's Essays, p. 185.

Note LXXXV.   Page 88.

Italienische Reise (edition of 1840 of Goethe's works), xxiv. 92.

Note LXXXVI.   Page 89.

Ibid., p. 79.

Note LXXXVII.   Page 90.

Passavant's Raphael, i. 552.

Note LXXXVIII.   Page 91.

Cf. Longhena, Istoria della Vita e delle Opere di Raffaello Sanzio da Urbino, del Sig. Quatremère de Quincy, ecc. (Milan, 1829), p. 657. (Cf. Passavant, i. 226, where, moreover, Misserini is erroneously written.)

Note LXXXIX.   Page 91.

Passavant, iii. 35.

Note XC.   Page 91.

Le Vite, p. 560.

Note XCI.   Page 92.

Preussische Jahrbücher, February 1864, p. 170.

Note XCII. Page 93.

Cf. Passavant, i. p. 225.

Note XCIII. Page 94.

Ibid., p. 226.

Note XCIV. Page 94.

Ibid., iii. p. 36.

Note XCV. Page 94.

Le Vite, pp. 554–555.

Note XCVI. Page 100.

Ibid., p. 559.

Note XCVII. Page 101.

Ibid., p. 560, note i. Le Monnier warmly refutes this in the Florentine edition of Vasari (1846).

Note XCVIII. Page 102.

Cf. Preussische Jahrbücher, January 1864, pp. 25–26.

Note XCIX. Page 102.

The inscription may be thus translated : ' To God, the all-powerful, the all-wise. To Maria Bibbiena, daughter of Antonio, his bride, who was snatched away by death from a happy union, who before her bridal torches were kindled, quitted this earth as a virgin, to her, the all-worthy, is this monument erected by Balthasar Turini of Pescia, the datary of Leo X., and John Baptist Branconio of Aquila, papal chamberlain, according to the testament placed under the care of Hieronymus Vagnini of Urbino, a relation of Raphael's, who also enlarged the chapel out of his own fortune' (cf. Pas_savant, i. 324–325, 559, where the Latin text is inserted). On the other hand, the editors of Vasari remark (p. 560, sect. i. note i. of the Trieste edition) that Pungileoni, in the Elogio di Raffaello, p. 166, in contradiction to the inscrip_tion ('invece'), speaks of Marietta, the daughter of Pietro, a natural brother of the ecclesiastical dignitary (that is, of Cardinal Bibbiena), who was married in 1515 to the Urbino noble and treasurer of the papal army, Bernardino Peruli, with a dowry of 5,000 gold scudi. If, however, we examine the passage in Pungileoni more accurately, we readily per-ceive that the editors have assigned a false meaning to it. Pungileoni says nothing more than (beginning at p. 165) : ' È cosa narrata le mille volte, che il cardinale Divizio da Bibiena gli (that is Raphael) offerse in isposa *Maria, figlia di suo nipote Antonio*; ma niuno si è dato il pensiero d'indagare in qual anno gliene facesse la non disgradita esibizione (in what year he made him the not rejected proposal). Una lettera trovata fra le scritture del duca d'Urbino Francesco Maria secondo, da lui, finchè visse, custodite con la maggior gelosia, ne accerta che Raffaello era disposto ad accettarla per donna ; che gliene aveva fatto solenne promessa coll' assenso degli zii paterno e materno ; che aveva ricusati più altri vantaggiosi partiti, ecc. Poi dove rinnovargliela nel 1515, allorche *Marietta, figlia di Pietro*, fratello carnale del Por-porato, venne sposata con dote di cinque mila scudi d'oro in oro di camera a Bernardino Peruli,' &c. Where is there one word here that Pungileoni considers Marietta, the daughter of Pietro, identical with Maria, the daughter of Antonio ? Where is there one word that, from the contents of a letter found among the papers of the duke of Urbino, he

aims at a refutation of the inscription on the monument of
Maria Bibbiena in the Pantheon? The passage from the
letter is merely given to fix the date more accurately when
the Cardinal Bibbiena offered his niece in marriage to
Raphael. The 'Poi dove (= dovette) rinnovargliela nel
1515, *allorche*,' &c., only means, afterwards, in 1515, *at the
same time* that Marietta married Peruli, he (that is, Raphael)
had to repeat it (that is, the solemn promise, 'solenne promessa,' to marry Maria). How could it be more plainly
expressed that Marietta and Maria were not identical; that
Pungileoni intended nothing but to furnish a proof that in
1515, Raphael's connection with Maria was not at an end;
just as, at p. 167, he again shows that this was not the case
even in 1517? He there mentions a letter of Bartolomeo
Divizj, the eldest brother of the cardinal, written in the year
1517 to the Latin poet Giovenale, in which Raphael's name
again appears in connection with that of Bernardino (Peruli),
though to the former the epithet 'nostro' is added, 'per l'alta
riputazione ch' ei godeva, e per la lusinga di strignere *seco lui*
(= con lui) nodi di parentela indissolubili,' that is, to form
an indissoluble bond with him, the famous Raphael, both on
account of the high reputation he enjoyed, and from the
flattering nature of the connection. We see that all these
statements in no wise contradict the purport of the epitaph,
according to which Maria died before Raphael, as his
affianced; they would, indeed, be rather confirmatory to it if
Pungileoni could have succeeded in finding still further documents of the years 1517 to 1520 (the year in which Raphael
died), which would place the continuation of the attachment
up to the death of the betrothed beyond a doubt.

Note C.   Page 103.

Guhl, Künstlerbriefe, i. 122–123.

Note CI.   Page 105.

Augsburger Allgemeine Zeitung of July 30, 1857.

Note CII.   Page 105.

See Buchanan's Memoirs of Paintings (London, 1829), i. 295, in the possession of Mr. Edward Gray in London.

Note CIII.   Page 105.

See Passavant, iii. 111.   This supposition rests, however, only on a notice by Morelli (ii. 120) of an anonymous picture. No one has seen the picture, and it is therefore very probable that the painting sold by Valati was a speculation based on this fact.   It may possibly have been an old copy of the same date.   Such is the opinion of Dr. G. G. Parthey at Berlin.

Note CIV.   Page 107.

Valery, Voyages en Italie (Brussels, 1843), p. 461.

Note CV.   Page 107.

Passavant, iii. 115.

Note CVI.   Page 108.

Incomprehensibly enough, in the catalogue of the Pina-kothek, this picture is entered as the portrait of Raphael, a supposition which is based entirely on a false interpretation of the words of Vasari (cf. Le Vite, p. 548), 'ed a Bindo Altoviti fece il ritratto *suo* dove era giovane.'   Bottari wa the first who was deceived by the equivocal expression of Vasari; he was followed by Raphael Morghen, who, in his engraving of the picture, designated it as a portrait of Raphael, and even by Rumohr, the profound investigator of art; but the error was rectified in a letter published at Venice and Florence by 'the Cavaliere Tommaso Puccini, and subsequently by Wicar, Missirini, Fea, Moreni, and Ernst Förster. King Louis I. of Bavaria, as crown prince, purchased the magnificent picture in 1808 for 350 zechins from the Altoviti family in Florence. Cf. Deutsches Museum (1864), No. 19, p. 692–693.

Note CVII. Page 108.

This picture was at any rate some time ago still in the possession of Mr. R. J. Mackintosh, who purchased it at the sale of Samuel Rogers's collection, and kept it in a street out of St. James's in London. According to the latest information, however, the collection of Mr. Mackintosh no longer exists.

Note CVIII. Page 109.

For details, see Passavant, i. 213–215; ii. 150–152; iii. 116, 118.

Note CIX. Page 110.

Von Savigny, Geschichte des römischen Rechts im Mittelalter, iii. 624.

Note CX. Page 110.

Passavant, i. 196.

Note CXI. Page 111.

Von Rumohr, Ueber Rafael, p. 103.

Note CXII. Page 113.

Cf. with this Vischer's Æsthetik, ii. 480: 'Das Mittelalter ist in Darstellung von Thieren äusserst schwach, während selbst die unreife orientalische Phantasie im Alterthum es darin schon weit brachte; auch ein Rafael hat noch wenig Thierformsinn und macht schlechtere Pferde als selbst die alterthümlich hart gezeichneten in den alten etruskischen Gräbern, an denen doch selbst die schwierigsten Theile des Fusses . . . schon mit einem Verständniss gegeben sind, welches zeigt, wie viel Sinn für diese edle, ihrem eigenen Charakter so verwandte Thiergattung die alten Volker hatten.' (Cf. ibid. iii. 3, 658.)

Note CXIII. Page 116.

Von Rumohr, p. 123.

Note CXIV. Page 117.

See Grenzboten von 1863, No. 27, p. 32. Whether Campori is a marquis, as I have styled him according to my authority, I cannot assert with any certainty. There is no marquis on the title of the Italian paper I have since received.

Note CXV. Page 119.

Goethe's works (1840), xxxi. 41–42.

Note CXVI. Page 119.

Ibid. xxiii. 174.

Note CXVII. Page 120.

There is a thorough explanation of these in Waagen's pamphlet, Die Cartons von Rafael, in besonderer Beziehung auf die nach denselben gewirkten Teppiche in der Rotunde des königlichen Museums zu Berlin. (Berlin, 1860.)

Note CXVIII. Page 123.

Vischer, Æsthetik, iii. 1, 157 ; 3, 622, 628, *et seq.*

Note CXIX. Page 124.

Le Vite, p. 551.

Note CXX. Page 125.

Grenzboten von 1863, No. 27, p. 29.

Note CXXI. Page 126.

The work has passed through many editions; the first appeared at Venice in 1528; another at Lyons in 1553; a third, incomplete, appeared again at Venice in 1593, and one in Padua in 1733.

Note CXXII. Page 127.

His complete works were published at Venice in four volumes in 1729; separate volumes had already appeared much earlier at different places.

Note CXXIII. Page 127.

Passavant, ii. 292–293; iii. 132–133.

Note CXXIV. Page 128.

Ibid. iii. 180–181.

Note CXXV. Page 133.

Vischer, Æsthetik, iii. 3, 717, 718.

NOTE CXXVI. Page 135.

Cf. Christliches Kunstblatt (1864), No. 2, p. 22–23.

NOTE CXXVII. Page 135.

Goethe's works (1840), xxiv. 172–173.

NOTE CXXVIII. Page 136.

Le Vite, p. 554–555. These paintings, which are now much injured and retouched by Carlo Maratti, are described in detail in Grimm's Leben Michel Angelo (2nd edition, Hanover, 1864), pp. 316–322. The paintings consist of ten triangular compartments, two great ceiling paintings (the 'Council of the Gods' and the 'Marriage of Cupid and Psyche'), and fourteen Amorini in the lunettes between the arches. There is a paper also in the Recensionen und Mittheilungen über bildende Kunst (Vienna, 1864, No. 34, pp. 265–368), by Fr. W. Unger, entitled, 'Rafael's Amor und Psyche in der Farnesina,' which appears worthy of notice, because it is here shown that Raphael in no wise treated the subject *as a fable*, in the spirit of Apulejus, but *allegorically*, in the spirit of the ancient mythology, that is, as a struggle between earthly and heavenly love (Venus and Cupid).

NOTE CXXIX. Page 138.

Cf. Passavant, i. 230–233.

. NOTE CXXX. Page 138.

Lettere Pitt. xvi. 213.

NOTE CXXXI. Page 139.

Goethe's Werke (1840), xxxiii. 119.

NOTE CXXXII. Page 139.

Nagler, Rafael als Mensch und Künstler (Munich, 1836), p. 159.

NOTE CXXXIII. Page 140.

Von Rumohr, Ueber Rafael und sein Verhältniss zu den Zeitgenossen (Berlin and Stettin, 1831), p. 120.

NOTE CXXXIV. Page 140.

Cf. Recensionen und Mittheilungen über bildende Kunst (Vienna, 1862), No. 9, p. 154–159, in which I erroneously stated that Mr. Du Boulay purchased the picture in 1855 from the son of a Signore Landucci, who had died at Florence; the old Landucci, however, died at Pescia, and the picture was not taken to Florence till after his death, when Du Boulay at once purchased it, so that it was not at all known there. This interesting question is also thoroughly discussed by Ruland in his paper, ' Professor Schäffer on a copy of Rafael's St. Cecilia,' in the ' Fine Arts Quarterly Review' (London, May 1864), pp. 346–358.

NOTE CXXXV. Page 140.

Ibid. No. 11, p. 187–188.

NOTE CXXXVI. Page 141.

Passavant, iii. 124.

NOTE CXXXVII. Page 141.

Nagler, p. 160.

NOTE CXXXVIII. Page 142.

Goethe's Werke (1840), xxxi. 41–42.

NOTE CXXXIX. Page 143.

Passavant, iii. 188–189.

NOTE CXL. Page 144.

Le Vite, p. 502.

NOTE CXLI. Page 144.

Visconti (Istoria del Ritrovamento degli Spogli Mortali di Raffaello Sanzio [Rome, 1833], p. 80), has discovered this engraving in the Corsini Gallery in Rome, and by this rectified the confusion made by Pietro Ferrerio (Raccolta dei Palazzi di Roma, Tav. 15), Sandrart, Comolli, and others, between the Raphael palace and that of Giovanni Battista Branconio d'Aquila.

NOTE CXLII. Page 145.

Passavant, iii. 192–194.

NOTE CXLIII. Page 146.

Ibid. ii. 443.

NOTE CXLIV. Page 147.

Guhl, Künstlerbriefe, i. 131.

NOTE CXLV. Page 148.

Bartsch, Peintre Graveur, xiv. No. 534.

NOTE CXLVI. Page 148.

Passavant, i. 235–237. Guhl, i. 124–126.

NOTE CXLVII. Page 149.

Agosto Frate Giocondo was sub-architect of St. Peter's from

1514 to 1518; and, besides him, Raphael had an associate in Giuliano, and subsequently in Antonio da San Gallo.

NOTE CXLVIII. Page 149.

Guhl, Künstlerbriefe, i. 128–129.

NOTE CXLIX. Page 150.

Ibid. i. 133–134.

NOTE CL. Page 151.

See Passavant's Latin original, i. 549.

NOTE CLI. Page 152.

Guhl, Künstlerbriefe, i. 135–145, and Daniele Francesconi, Conjettura che una lettera creduta di Baldassare Castiglione sia di Raffaello d' Urbino (Florence, 1799).

NOTE CLII. Page 154.

Vasari, in his life of Fra Giocondo, describes Raphael's bold proceeding. Cf. Le Vite, p. 699.

NOTE CLIII. Page 155.

Le Vite, p. 553.

NOTE CLIV. Page 156.

Passavant, ii. 452, 453, 457.

NOTE CLV. Page 157.

Ibid. i. 253, 254.

NOTE CLVI.   Page 157.

Vischer, Æsthetik, iii. i. p. 326.

NOTE CLVII.   Page 158.

Lettere Pittor., vol. v. No. 5, p. 245.

NOTE CLVIII.   Page 158.

The Penny Magazine of July 17, 1841, has a copy of this in a woodcut.

NOTE CLIX.   Page 158.

Cavaceppi, Raccolta d' antiche Statue, plate i. 44 ; and Passavant, ii. 438–440.

NOTE CLX.   Page 158.

Passavant, iii. 33–34, and 183–184.

NOTE CLXI.   Page 158.

Müller, Ein Kupferstich von Rafael (Düsseldorf, 1860).

NOTE CLXII.   Page 160.

Le Vite, p. 549.   ' Avendo dunque veduto Raffaello lo andare nelle stampe d' Alberto Dürero, volonteroso ancor egli di mostrare quel che in tale arte poteva, fece studiare Marco Antonio Bolognese in questa pratica infinamente.'   (Cf. Nagler, Künstlerlexikon, xii. 207.)

NOTE CLXIII.   Page 162.

Dolce, Dialogo della Pittura (styled l' Aretina, because P. Aretino furnished Dolce with the materials for it) (Venice, 1557–8), p. 24.

Note CLXIV.　Page 162.

Passavant, vol. ii. Nos. 82, 83, p. 475.

Note CLXV.　Page 163.

Von Rumohr, Italienische Forschungen, iii. 117.

Note CLXVI.　Page 166.

Notizie Inedite di Raffaello da Urbino.　Grenzboten von 1863, No. 27, p. 27–28.

Note CLXVII.　Page 166.

Cf. the letters from Goro Gheri in Rome to Baldassare Turini in Florence, in Gaye's Carteggio inedito d' Artisti dei secoli 14–16, vol. ii. Nos. 90, 91.　(Passavant, ii. 139–140.)

Note CLXVIII.　Page 167.

Le Vite (Vita di Giulio Romano), p. 759.

Note CLXIX.　Page 167.

André Félibien, Entretiens sur les Vies et les Ouvrages des plus excellents Peintres anciens et modernes (Paris, 1666), ii. 335.

Note CLXX.　Page 167.

Passavant, ii. 317–320.

Note CLXXI.　Page 168.

Von Rumohr, Italienische Forschungen, iii. 129, and Drei Reisen nach Italien, p. 78.

Note CLXXII.　Page 169.

Le Vite, p. 554.

Note CLXXIII. Page 169.

Thus it stands in the catalogue of the Dresden Gallery in 1862, p. 131; but Winckelmann in a letter to Berendis, September 17, 1754, states the sum to have been 5,000*l*., without the cost of transport. Cf. Passavant, i. 340.

Note CLXXIV. Page 169.

Böttiger, Artistisches Notizenblatt (1825), No. 24.

Note CLXXV. Page 169.

Ibid. (1826), No. 1.

Note CLXXVI. Page 170.

Vischer, Æsthetik, iii. 3, 619.

Note CLXXVII. Page 172.

I have in these remarks endeavoured to give a short résumé of an article well worthy of notice, entitled, ' Die Künstlerische Anordnung von Rafael's Sixtinischer Madonna,' contributed by Riegel to the Morgenblatt of 1864, No. 24, pp. 558–563. A woodcut which is there given shows the mathematical laws which he has followed with so much exactness.

Note CLXXVIII. Page 172.

Vischer, Æsthetik, iii. 3, 619.

Note CLXXIX. Page 172.

Heucking, ' Die Sixtinische Madonna. In ihrer sittlichen Wirkung ausgelegt und erklärt.' (Petersburg, 1862.)

Note CLXXX.   Page 174.

Blätter für literarische Unterhaltung (Leipsic, 1863), No. 20, p. 370.

Note CLXXXI.   Page 177.

Goethe's Werke (1840), xxiv. 170–171.

Note CLXXXII.   Page 178.

Ibid. (1840), xxxi. 43–49, 'Ueber Christus und die zwölf Apostel.'

Note CLXXXIII.   Page 179.

Ibid. xxiv. 167.

Note CLXXXIV.   Page 181.

Le Vite, p. 560.

Note CLXXXV.   Page 181.

Pungileoni, Elogio storico di Raffaello Santi, p. 246, relates, according to the statement of Melchior Missirini, that Raphael was suddenly summoned to the Pope, on account of some affair of importance, and in consequence arrived very much heated; that he then had a long conversation with him in a drafty room, and caught his fatal illness from the chill he then received.

Note CLXXXVI.   Page 181.

Le Vite, p. 554.

Note CLXXXVII.   Page 182.

Grenzboten von 1863, No. 27, p. 20. Pungileoni also, in his Elogio storico di Raffaello Santi, p. 246, speaks of a fever, which, ' in pochi dì,' ended fatally, in spite of all the remedies applied. Vasari's editors (Le Monnier's Florentine edition of 1846 ; Trieste edition, p. 560, section 2, note 2) say that his illness lasted fifteen days, and that during this time he received from all sides, and even from the Pope himself, the warmest proofs of the most hearty sympathy.

NOTE CLXXXVIII. Page 184.

Le Vite, p. 561.

NOTE CLXXXIX. Page 185.

Passavant, i. 325–327.

NOTE CXC. Page 186.

Le Vite, p. 560.

NOTE CXCI. Page 188.

Braun, Disputa, p. 154.'

NOTE CXCII. Page 188.

Ibid. p. 154.

NOTE CXCIII. Page 189.

Vischer, Æsthetik, iii. 713, 714.

NOTE CXCIV. Page 195.

Macaulay's History of England, i. 44.

NOTE CXCV. Page 196.

Vischer, Æsthetik, iii. 3, 712, 713.

NOTE CXCVI.   Page 197.

Vischer, Æsthetik, iii. p. 717.

NOTE CXCVII.   Page 199.

Especial stress must be laid upon this fact, for too often the influence of the antique upon Raphael's art is represented as too sudden and direct; he felt its influence, however, in the atmosphere of the entire age of the Renaissance, in poets and writers, such as Dante, Petrarca, Boccaccio, Frezzi (the author of the ' Quadriregio '), Lorenzo Valla, Flavio Biondo, Bernardo Ruccellai (the first Roman antiquarian), and many others; he felt its influence above all, as regards plastic art, in the purity of the Florentine form, which already contained in itself the spirit of the antique, and from which Raphael drew, before he had reached the fount of the antique.

NOTE CXCVIII.   Page 201.

Cf. Gruyer, Raphael et l'Antiquité (Paris, 1864), i. 224–225; ii. 409–419.   I will not assert that Raphael reached Phidias's ideal of beauty; perhaps he approaches closer to Praxiteles than to Phidias, who has ever been enthroned in solitary grandeur.   But, in spite of this, Gruyer was right in his assertion; for, judging by what later classic art had until then produced, Raphael alone and no other can be placed by the side of Phidias as the representative of modern art.   Still the question whether it will ever be possible to bring Phidias's true ideal of beauty into harmony with our modern knowledge is perhaps connected with that other question, whether a great art-epoch is at all to be expected or no.   Those who proclaim a still higher future for the human race will answer this latter question in the affirmative.

Note CXCIX. Page 202.

Goethe's Werke (1840), xxx. 467.

Note CC. Page 202.

Von Schadow, Ueber den Einfluss des Christenthums auf die bildende Kunst. A Lecture (Düsseldorf, 1842), p. 6.

Note CCI. Page 206.

These are Overbeck's own words in a letter written by him from Aricia, near Rome, on September 3, 1857, to the engraver Ludy, at Berlin. Both designs were made by Overbeck at an early period for a Counsellor Reimer (the bookseller or his brother) at Berlin, as companion pictures, and Ludy engraved them in 1859, with the permission of the artist, for the publisher Manz at Ratisbon, in cartoon fashion, or, as the French call it, ' manière blonde ou allemande.' Overbeck himself sets especial value on the ' Expulsion of Hagar.' This composition was originally in a triangular form, and this first original is in the possession of a Miss Auguste Klein; in the design for Reimer it is in a square form. Ludy, who is well qualified for the task, has engraved many of Overbeck's paintings, the greater part of which have been published by Schulgen and Schwann in Paris. All his works are distinguished by great depth of feeling and elegance.

Note CCII. Page 207.

Vischer, Æsthetik, iii. 3, 750.

Note CCIII. Page 207.

Ibid. p. 751.

. Note CCIV.   Page 209.

Vischer, Æsthetik, iii. p. 713.

·Note CCV.   Page 210.

Die Illustrirte Welt (Stuttgart, 1864), part i. pp. 4–7. 'Das Juwel der Dresdener Gallerie.'

Note CCVI. · Page 217.

Vischer, Æsthetik, ii. 391.

INDEX

LONDON
PRINTED BY SPOTTISWOODE AND CO.
NEW-STREET SQUARE

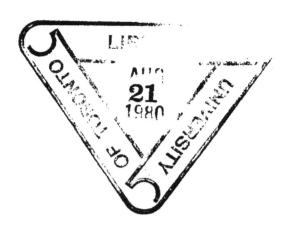

BY THE SAME TRANSLATOR.

SHAKESPEARE COMMENTARIES.
 By Dr. G. G. Gervinus, Professor at Heidelberg.
 2 vols. demy 8vo. 24*s*.

LIFE OF MICHAEL ANGELO.
 By Herman Grimm. With Photographic Portrait from
 the Picture in the Vatican. Second Edition. 2 vols.
 crown 8vo. 24*s*.

London: SMITH, ELDER, & CO., 65 Cornhill.

Lightning Source UK Ltd.
Milton Keynes UK
UKHW05f1210080818
326899UK00021B/622/P